# TURNING POINTS

Cover Image: Jonas Jungblut/Workbook Stock/Getty

Published by Barbour Publishing, Inc., P.O. Box 719, Uhrichsville, Ohio 44683
www.barbourbooks.com

*Our mission is to publish and distribute inspirational products offering exceptional value and biblical encouragement to the masses.*

Member of the
Evangelical Christian
Publishers Association

Printed in the United States of America.

# TURNING POINTS

Janice Hanna
Kathleen Y'Barbo

I Know
I'm Not Alone,
Lord

Rediscovering Joy and
Contentment after Divorce

BARBOUR
PUBLISHING

*To all of my newly single sisters. . .*
*On the tail end of every sorrow, may you find a joyful tomorrow!*
JANICE

*To Jan Freeman and Buddy Riddle at the Met Church for leading*
*the way when I could barely find my feet and follow, and to DiAnn*
*Mills for pointing me to them—and to God. Thanks to You, I'm still*
*standing. Without You, this book—and the continuing story of my*
*life—would never have been written.*
KATHLEEN

## ACKNOWLEDGMENTS

To Paul Looney, Christian psychiatrist and awesome friend. Paul, we are so grateful for your input. Your words of wisdom will help many who read this book. We're also thankful that you choose to spend countless hours walking wounded people through the necessary healing after life's traumas. May God richly bless your labors.

To Nancy Williams, life coach and dear friend. What can we say? You are our sister, our mentor, our advisor, and our friend. You are a beacon, guiding those you coach out of darkness and into His marvelous light. Bless you again and again for helping with this book—and congratulations on your own upcoming book! We're so proud of you!

To Beverly Blackstone, personal counselor, therapist, spiritual lightning rod, and all-around awesome woman of God. We have both leaned on you in good times and bad. Thank you for your contribution to this difficult—but necessary—project. You know from whence you speak. May God continue to use you to bring life and hope to others through the Water's Edge Ministry.

To Jay Meyers, wonderful counselor and an example to many— thank you for your comments! We're so grateful. We pray God's richest blessings on your counseling ministry and your wife's as well.

# CONTENTS

A Note from the Authors.......................... 6

Overview.......................................... 7

Introduction ..................................... 9

Chapter 1: *You Are Not Alone* .................... 15

Chapter 2: *The Shock Period*..................... 37

Chapter 3: *Oh, Those Changes!* .................. 61

Chapter 4: *Dealing with Fear* ................... 83

Chapter 5: *The Deep Stuff* ...................... 105

Chapter 6: *It's All about Choices* .............. 129

Chapter 7: *Calgon, Take Me Away!* ............... 149

Chapter 8: *Content in Him* ...................... 173

Chapter 9: *Leaning on God*....................... 195

# A Note from the Authors

Dear Reader,

   If you've been through the heartbreak of divorce, we want you to know this book was written specifically for you. . .by two Christian women who've walked many a mile in your shoes. You are not alone! Contemplate that for a moment. The ups and downs you've experienced during this season of your life have been shared—not just by the two of us, but by millions of other women. And yet these women, for the most part, feel lost. Confused. Alone. Well, no more! The Lord desires that his daughters walk in victory and in strength. There is nothing that can hold you back when you're a child of the King. Divorce is a detour, not the end of the road. The Lord has amazing plans for you!

*If one dream should fall and break into a thousand pieces,*
*never be afraid to pick one of those pieces up and begin again.*
Flavia Weedn

# OVERVIEW

The words of this book are bathed in prayer and were written with you in mind. They are divided into nine chapters, each specifically dealing with a particular subject divorced women face. Each chapter is divided into five sections:

- *Face It:* a section for the reader to take a look at the particular issue being addressed and acknowledge it for what it is in her life.
- *Grace It:* taking a look at the chapter's issue through the filter of grace. This section includes a written prayer for the reader to participate in.
- *Erase It:* a section for the reader to erase any negative attitudes or feelings she's struggling with regarding that issue.
- *Replace It:* a section loaded with biblically based advice to help women overcome that particular issue.
- *Embrace It:* final words of encouragement to point the reader toward the One with the answers. Let the adventure begin!

We pray that you are able to read through this book with a happy heart, ready for a great adventure ahead. May your journey be all you dreamed. . .and more!

# Introduction

*But as for you, you meant evil against me;
but God meant it for good.*
GENESIS 50:20 NKJV*

There is life after divorce.

Maybe you needed to hear those words. They offer such hope, don't they? If you've gone through the unexpected challenge of divorce, you need to know that life will go on. In fact, you can celebrate a thriving, happy life. . .not in spite of what you've been through, but because of it. This is not the end of the road for you. No, it is truly the beginning of an amazing new chapter in your life—one filled with pages yet to be written.

There are two distinctly different ways that divorce can affect us. Let's use the analogy of a house to explain. Imagine your dream home complete with lovely landscaping, pool, and, of course, family photos on the wall.

For some women, divorce will feel like an explosion, like your cherished home suddenly and unexpectedly blows up without any prior warning. All you're left with are the shattered pieces. Around you are shards of glass, the tattered fabric of the bedroom curtains, and perhaps a few burnt and barely recognizable toys from the playroom. There's no way to know where anything went or how to put it all together again. You wander around in a daze with nowhere to rest and nothing but debris as far as you can see. It is, in short, a disaster area of epic proportions with no hope for the Red Cross to appear and take away the suffering.

For others, it happens more slowly, perhaps taking years. Imagine one room of your home being hit by a falling tree. You seal off that room and live only in the others. Then imagine a meteor falling from the sky and landing on another room. You seal it off and continue to live in a smaller space. Then a tornado hits and takes out another room. And the storms keep coming. Each time something catastrophic happens in the marriage (infidelity, betrayal, etc.) another room gets destroyed, then sealed off. Eventually, the whole family is huddled together in one small closet, unable to breathe. In desperation and defeat, one of the parties decides there's only one thing that makes sense: divorce.

Maybe you never figured you'd be in the position you're in right now. In fact, if you're like most women, you probably had your "happily ever after" planned out from childhood and never allotted for any kinks. A divorce decree was likely not something you thought of on your wedding day, nor did you plan for a life of singleness while plotting your fairy tale ending.

Oh, daughter of God! There is such good news! With your heavenly Father in control, you will still have that happily-ever-after. In this story, a Knight on a white horse will rush in and save the fair damsel in distress. And if you use your imagination, you can almost see yourself facing a brighter future than ever before.

Perhaps it's too soon to consider such a thing. Maybe you've decided happiness is something you left back in your marriage, never to be recaptured. For now, set those fears aside and see what the Lord says to you as you journey through these pages. You just might be surprised at the result.

Before we look ahead, it's important to take at least one glimpse back at what led you here. Maybe your story is a little like Cindy's.

Cindy always loved weddings. She played bride, orchestrated dollhouse weddings, and made veils for herself using her mother's white pillowcases, all before she was old enough to spell her name. She started planning her own wedding when she was eight years old. By the time she reached high school, she'd pasted pictures from magazines onto her walls, chosen her dress and veil, named her bridesmaids, written her vows, and planned the menu for the reception. The cake would be white, multi-layered, with fresh flowers adorning the table; the ring, a perfect round cut with side stones; and the music would include a collection of songs she'd been adding to since childhood. Cindy had even picked out her dream spot for a honeymoon: an all-inclusive beach resort on a warm Caribbean island. All she needed was a groom.

Her freshman year in college, Cindy met the man of her dreams. He was everything she'd prayed for, as was the engagement that happened the summer before their senior year. Plans for the big wedding soon kicked into high gear with silver patterns nudging out schoolbooks for Cindy's attention. They married just after graduation, each joyously committing to the relationship, "till death do us part."

In short order, they had 2.5 children, purchased a dog, moved into a house with a white picket fence, and began to acquire credit card debt. The family went on vacations together and practically took up residence in their minivan as they shuffled the kids back and forth from ballet lessons to soccer practice, from karate to choir practice. They joined a local church, where Cindy worked in the women's ministry and her husband taught Sunday school. They attended parties and retreats together and were the couple to be envied—at least on the surface.

Inside the walls of the home, however, things weren't as happy-go-lucky as they appeared. Cindy and her husband went through the usual ups and downs, but faced some unforeseen challenges beyond the norm. Betrayal, hurt, and unforgiveness reared their ugly heads. Those things led to major shifts in attitudes and actions; and before long, things began to unravel. Cindy did her best to pray, to do the right things and stand by her man. But believing in God's intervention didn't change the fact that, in the end, a judge—a total stranger to Cindy—banged his gavel, and made his pronouncement. Her happily-ever-after, as she knew it, came to a grinding halt. What took years to build ended in a moment.

Cindy walked out of the courthouse a single woman for the first time in years. She put her wedding ring in the back of her jewelry box and squared her shoulders, trying to ignore the place on her finger where the skin was slightly less tanned. In that moment, as she closed the jewelry box lid, she determined to make the best of things. What else could she do, after all? There was no going backward in time; she could only go forward. Sure, Cindy occasionally pondered the "till death do us part" thing, especially on days when it felt like her hope had died. . .that her faith was small and her dreams impossible. But she refused to give up.

Over the following weeks and months, she put one foot in front of the other and took baby steps toward an unknown future. Changes occurred, and she dealt with each as she could manage it: putting the house on the market, finding a new place, helping the kids adapt to new schools, learning to live on a reduced income, and so much more. Through the haze of emotions, she could barely make out the road ahead.

In between bouts of grief, she felt a sense of adventure about the journey; but at times, fear loomed large. Choices beckoned, and she struggled to make the right decisions. Everyday things—like broken toilets and leaky faucets—threatened to be her undoing. And contentment. . .well, contentment was now a word she found herself using only in the past tense. When she saw it in others, she barely remembered what it felt like.

Cindy faced an ever-growing identity crisis. She couldn't figure out who she was without a husband in the picture. All of her life, she'd been wife and mother. Now. . .who was she? Was she defective? Unlovable? When would things just return to normal so that she would know how to act? With her emotions in a whirlwind, she felt as if she might very well come unraveled. What would be left of her, once life slowed down?

Can you relate to Cindy's story? Do you feel your happily-ever-after was torn from your hands? That your ideal life was stripped away and replaced with a life that feels unfamiliar and strange? If so, then you're in good company. Hundreds of thousands of Christian women have walked this road before you, and, with God's help, have created new and lasting relationships. . .with the Lord, with their children, and with their friends. Many have even moved on into new marriages, applying the lessons they've learned from the mistakes of the past.

Isn't it consoling to know the Lord has plans for your life? "'For I know the plans I have for you,' declares the LORD, 'plans to prosper you and not to harm you, plans to give you hope and a future' " (Jeremiah 29:11 NIV). Notice the verse doesn't speak of a singular plan. Our creative God has plans (plural) for your life. And what hopeful, positive ones they are!

So, maybe you took a wrong turn. Or maybe someone else's actions forced you to the place you are now. Maybe you were a strong advocate for your marriage, but your mate was not. Likely you both made a few mistakes along the way. Regardless, the same God who created the heavens and the earth will meet you right where you are and lead you down a road filled with peace and joy. What the enemy meant for evil, God will use for good in your life. . .if you let Him. The choice is up to you.

Yes, there is life after divorce. And better still. . .it can be a good one!

*There is in every true woman's heart a spark of heavenly fire, which lies dormant in the broad daylight of prosperity; but which kindles up, and beams and blazes in the dark hour of adversity.*
WASHINGTON IRVING

# Chapter 1

## *You Are Not Alone*

*I have woven a parachute out of everything broken.*
WILLIAM STAFFORD

## ◠ FACE IT

You are not alone.

Maybe you read those words and say, "Really? Well, I sure *feel* alone." Sometimes physical aloneness can cause us to feel like we've been abandoned on every level. As believers, we understand that God is with us at all times; but without that other flesh-and-blood person sitting next to us, it's easy to forget He's there. We're overcome by feelings we can't seem to control. And just about the time we manage to get them under control, something else happens to remind us that we're no longer married.

You feel alone at times. Go ahead. Admit it. It's impossible to get beyond something without acknowledging it. You have to face the unexpected things of life head-on. You never planned to get divorced. Unfortunately, things didn't go as you planned. For whatever reason, you are now a single woman once again.

Maybe you hear the word *single* and shudder. Maybe you think you can't make it alone. What a relief to discover you don't have to! The Word of God promises that you are never alone: "'Never will I leave you; never will I forsake you' " (Hebrews 13:5 NIV). Maybe you're trying to reconcile the two concepts in your mind. *I'm alone physically. I'm never alone spiritually.*

Remember Cindy, from our previous story? She was one of those women who never pictured herself without a man in her life. Ever. Stepping out into singlehood was new, frightening. She had relied on her husband to handle a great many things: the bills, things around the house, bank accounts. And now, trying to tackle those things on her own, feelings of abandonment kicked in.

Cindy struggled with feelings of aloneness, particularly when crawling into bed at night. In fact, those feelings consumed her at times. When she contemplated the word *alone*, she often realized just how alone she'd felt in her marriage. But this was different. The empty pillow next to her served as a constant reminder. And the extra chair at the kitchen table didn't help, either.

But what is it about being alone that scares us? After all, God often calls us to seasons of aloneness to draw us close to Him. Why do we balk at the idea? Perhaps because it's a strange, unfamiliar place for the newly single woman. For years, we had that other person next to us. And figuring out how to "do life" without him is sure to be a challenge. Like every challenge, you have to face it. Deal with it. Conquer it.

Consider these words from Christian psychiatrist, Dr. Paul Looney:

> *If change is difficult, unwanted change is even more troubling. When thrust into a circumstance not of our choosing, our feelings of helplessness and powerlessness grow. Particularly for women who go from their parents' house to marriage, being alone can seem terrifying. Even women who are highly successful and have been carrying the weight of finances in a marriage can feel very unsure about surviving as a single woman.*
>
> *No matter how bright and competent you are, you may struggle with fear until you establish some history of self-sufficiency. When we are married, it is easy to let our spouse be the keeper of our hearts. We can lean on them for our*

*security and sense of peace. If we are not careful, our mate
can function as a rival god. Many women I've worked with
in counseling found, through divorce, how to let God be God.*

Letting God be God isn't always easy, is it? It's especially tough
when we can't see, feel, or hear Him. Still, allowing Him to
take His rightful place is exactly the antidote for the pain of
aloneness. Only when we allow Him to fully "be" God can we
sense His nearness. That's why it's so important to deal with
what we're feeling head-on.

So, when does the aloneness bother you most? Maybe you
climb into bed at night and miss that warm body next to you.
Or perhaps you sit in a Sunday school class without a spouse
beside you and sense the aloneness more than ever. Chances
are, you've struggled at church, in restaurants, at family events,
on vacations, or even when you're holding the remote control,
realizing there's no one to snatch it from you.

That feeling of aloneness is especially pronounced when the
bill collectors are calling, when things in your home need repair,
when health issues crop up, or when a shelf needs to be nailed
back to the wall. Perhaps there's a light bulb you can't change
because it is out of reach, or a jar lid that just won't budge.
The everyday things—a flat tire, a broken fence, loading the
dishwasher with fewer dishes than before—can wreak havoc on
your emotions. And the big stuff? When you face the devastating
loss of a parent or family member without a spouse at your side?
There's no denying it. These things are harder without a husband
holding your hand.

And yet. . .

We serve a God of the impossible. If you don't believe it, take a look at the Old Testament stories once again. Walls of Jericho? Tumbled to the ground. (Was Joshua alone?) The mighty Goliath? Taken out by a kid with a slingshot. (Was David alone?) Pharaoh and his fast-moving army? Swallowed up by the Red Sea. (Was Moses alone?)

God delights in doing the impossible. And while our current situations might not be as staggering as the obstacles faced by Old Testament saints, God has not changed. He's the same yesterday, today, and tomorrow. He is able. . .and He is willing.

The Word of God is full of promises made to you, God's child. And your heavenly Father is *not* a promise breaker. "God is not a man, that He should lie, nor a son of man, that He should repent; has He said, and will He not do it? Or has He spoken, and will He not make it good?" (Numbers 23:19 NASB). He has promised He will never leave you nor forsake you. You can bank on that. "Keep your lives free from the love of money and be content with what you have, because God has said, 'Never will I leave you; never will I forsake you'" (Hebrews 13:5 NIV). When you go through the floodwaters—and you will—God is with you. You can even go through the fire and come out without the smell of smoke in your hair. "'When you pass through the waters, I will be with you; and when you pass through the rivers, they will not sweep over you. When you walk through the fire, you will not be burned; the flames will not set you ablaze'" (Isaiah 43:2 NIV). You can learn to lean on the Lord, even with the empty pillow next to you at night.

Hard to believe right now? It won't always be. Someday you will look back and see all the places where the Lord led you through. Or perhaps in the times your aloneness was so overpowering, the only reason you made it was because He carried you.

With God's help, you will make it! And remember. . ."that which doesn't kill us makes us stronger."

## GRACE IT

When you go through "alone" times, it's often hard to see that Jesus is right there next to you. During your weakest moments, He offers grace to bring you strength. Ponder the words of 2 Corinthians 12:9 from the King James version: "And he said unto me, My grace is sufficient for thee: for my strength is made perfect in weakness. Most gladly therefore will I rather glory in my infirmities, that the power of Christ may rest upon me."

Think about that. Paul actually gloried in his infirmities. He didn't spend time kicking himself for having troubles. Instead, he leaned on the grace of God, which was more than enough to see him through. That same grace will strengthen you in your weak times, too.

*Lord, I'm so ready to admit that I feel alone. And weak. I know in my heart that You are standing right there next to me, and I ask that Your presence be more real to me than ever before. Thank You for your grace, Lord. I'm so*

*grateful that You continue to pour it out during my weakest
moments that I may be strong in You. It is an ever-present
reminder that I am never truly alone. Amen.*

# C ERASE IT

> *Life is 10 percent of what happens to me
> and 90 percent of how I react to it.*
> JOHN MAXWELL

Whew! It feels good to acknowledge your feelings, doesn't it?
And it feels even better to know you're never truly alone. But
now what?

It's time to get specific. To figure out when you're struggling
most. . .and what to do about it. After all, the Lord wants to see
you healed and whole, and that only comes if you take action.

Take a look at the list below. Pause a few minutes and ask
the Lord to reveal the times and places you feel most vulnerable.
As you spend time in prayer, individually address each time or
place, asking the Lord to show you ways to feel His presence
while there.

I feel most alone:

- In restaurants
- At church
- In Sunday school

- In bed
- While paying bills
- When my friends are talking about their marriages
- In the car
- Watching television
- During family celebrations or big events
- When the children are with their father
- At weddings
- During a crisis
- When looking at friends' family photos
- At my children's soccer games, ballet recitals, or other events
- When the car needs work
- When contemplating a vacation
- When something in the house needs repair
- During the holidays
- On weekends
- When dealing with parenting issues, big or small

As you pray about the situations where you feel most alone, ask the Lord to give you other ideas for how you can turn that aloneness into a positive thing. For example, bedtime is a great time for book reading. Family celebrations provide the perfect opportunity to invite a best friend along. (She will make you feel at ease.) Many restaurants are now set up with wireless Internet access. If you own a laptop, take it with you and catch up on e-mails or work. Or, take along a good book. If your church doesn't already have a ministry to assist single women (helping with things like car repair), ask them to start one.

Realizing that the feelings of aloneness come along when you're *not* alone will help you feel less surprised when they surface during times spent with your children. The same goes for weddings, soccer games, and ballet recitals. These are all places where you might want to bring a friend. Or better yet, step out in faith and make new friends by introducing yourself to the moms you might not know. You'd be surprised how many married women feel just as alone as you in situations such as that.

Consider Meg's story:

*After my husband left, it was just my toddler daughter and me and our two dogs. I felt alone at times, but I wasn't really. I knew that God was with me. I was desperate for Him and poured out my heart to Him every night and often throughout the day. He gave me peace, which I so desperately needed at that time.*

*I also had an extensive support network—something I know that most single moms do not have—and I didn't take it for granted. I had my family and friends—all of whom were confused by my ex-husband's behavior and sad for me and for my daughter. Friends would provide a listening ear and sometimes do practical things like little handyman-stuff around the house. (That was a huge help!)*

*My parents, sister, sister-in-law, and a close friend babysat for me when I needed a break or had a work- or church-related event to attend. I had online writing buddies who reached out to me through e-mail and provided*

*encouragement and professional advice throughout. I was
fortunate in the number of people around; yet, as you know,
divorce and single parenthood is something you carry by
yourself. I knew that God was holding me close and holding
me up when I felt like giving up. Without His presence and
strength, I would not have made it through the pain and
fear of the unknown.*

Can you relate to Meg's words? Keeping your eyes open
for positive ways to approach your singleness is part of the
challenge, but it can also open you up to new friends and
experiences you might never have had. So ask God to remove
the negative feelings and show you His responses. Then step out
in faith with the assurance that while you may be alone, you do
not have to feel lonely.

In short. . .take action!

## ☾ REPLACE IT

> *He maketh me to lie down in green pastures:*
> *he leadeth me beside the still waters.*
> PSALM 23:2 KJV

You've acknowledged your feelings of aloneness and have even
gotten specific with God about where and when you feel most
alone. You've asked Him to erase those feelings. Now it's time to

replace them. We're going to start by reexamining "aloneness." God wants you to replace your "I can't stand to be alone" feelings with "I love being alone with Him."

Throughout history, God has called his people to periods of alone time to draw them closer to Him. Moses had his Tent of Meeting. David had his green pastures. The disciples had the upper room. In short, each person had his or her place (or opportunity) to get alone with God. To seek His will.

Even Jesus needed to get away from the crowd. Didn't He go into the wilderness before starting His ministry? Didn't He seek out a place in the Garden of Gethsemane to retreat from His disciples? Like the disciples in the upper room, He needed—and wanted—a set-apart place to spend intimate, quality time with His heavenly Father.

Your situation is no different. If you ever needed to know God's will—if you ever needed to get His perspective, His plan—it's now. So, don't fear the alone time with Him. It is a gift. Meet with God today. And tomorrow. And the next day. And all the days after that, whether you're single or married. You need God's input in your life, not just because of your situation but because you're a child of the King and He longs to spend quality one-on-one time with you.

In that secret, quiet place, God is sure to change your fear of the unknown into a sense of wonder. "I wonder what God is going to do" will become your new catchphrase. And, as you meet with Him, that sense of wonder will stir up an anticipation of how God is going to minister to you in your aloneness. No longer will you run from it. Instead, you will draw close and ask questions, such as: "Where are we going next, God?" "How are You going to handle this problem?" "What exciting things are You going to reveal to me today?"

This aloneness is a journey filled with adventure at every turn! And it's something we *get* to do, not something we *have* to do. In our one-on-one time with the Lord, we can think more clearly. Make better decisions. See the road ahead a little clearer. We meet with Him to get clarity and vision for the road ahead.

Without a doubt, God draws you to seasons of aloneness. And it's important we see these seasons in perspective. However, He does not intend for his daughters to hide away, keeping themselves from people, places, and things. The Lord placed us in communities so that we could both give and receive from one another. That's so critical to our survival and our growth.

So let's look at some specific things you can do to stay connected with the people around you during this season:

- **Get out of the house during the times (say, evenings) when you're most vulnerable.** There are so many ways to stay connected with others. Even the act of going to the grocery store can be used as a way to reconnect with people. Grab your cart and peruse the fresh vegetables or floral goods or spend some time checking out the latest magazines. Anything that gets you out of the house is a plus on days when you're tempted to pull the covers over your head and wallow in your aloneness.

- **Spend more time with your girlfriends.** It's also fun to reconnect with long-lost friends from high school and college. Women enjoy hanging out with other women, and there's no better time! In that mix of friends—new and old—you are bound to find a few who can connect with what you're going through. Don't know how to find these long-lost friends? With the advent of social networking sites such as Facebook and MySpace and reunion sites specific to your high school or college, reconnecting with old friends is easier than ever.

- **Join a Bible study.** If your local church doesn't have a strong women's ministry, then check around; some of the other churches in the community might. These Bible studies are often set up so that women from other churches can participate. Pick a study that works for you. For example, you're probably going to want to avoid the "How to Keep Your Marriage Strong" studies for now. Pick topics that meet you where you are. And trust that God knows what He's doing by placing you in the groups that He does.

- **Join your church choir (or begin to develop those other talents that might have been neglected for all those years).** Maybe you enjoyed singing, acting, cooking, painting, etc., when you were younger, but have let your dreams die. Pick them back up again! That's what Laurel did:

*During my divorce I began to ask God what I could do to fill these awful expanses of time I was left with. Television didn't cut it; and since my husband*

*and I had been avid moviegoers, watching films wasn't the best thing to take away thoughts of what I had lost. Then a friend suggested I join a quilting group. Me? I thought. And yet it did seem interesting to me even though I'd never attempted to quilt. After all, I owned many that had been passed down from my grandmother, so I did have an interest in them. To my surprise, the group was a varied bunch with as much wisdom and humor as quilting skills. I'm a ways down the road from the day I walked into the first meeting, and yet I still keep going. I may never become an expert quilter; but with every crooked stitch I take, I rejoice in how God has set me into a group of women who have marched with me every step of the way back to wholeness. I will also never have to worry about sleeping cold and alone, as I have any number of beautiful-to-me quilts I've created.*

- **Join a reader's club.** If you love to read, find other people in your area who are like-minded. Have monthly get-togethers and discuss what you're reading. Invite an author to speak to your group. Most can be contacted through their websites, and many offer discussion questions either in the back of their books or online.

- **Take classes at your local college.** You might just be surprised at the fun you'll have (and the things you'll learn). Nowadays classes with topics as wide-ranging as Conversational Spanish and Plumbing for Novices can be found. Perhaps you're looking to improve your job skills rather than your plumbing. Why not seek out a class on computers or technical writing, or maybe even find a certification in some new area? Most are available in evening and weekend classes and some can even be experienced through online learning. If you already have your bachelor's degree, why not pursue an advanced degree?

- **If you have a home-improvement supercenter or arts-and-crafts supply store in your area, check into their free classes.** Many offer a variety of lessons from the most basic how-tos to the more intricate skills, and some will even offer a discount on materials. You'll be a fix-it pro or arts-and-crafts expert in no time!

- **Journal.** Writing is cathartic. It's cleansing. If you've never journaled, this is a great time to start. The best thing about journaling is that it helps you now and later. Just ask Joan:

> *I started out writing in a journal that was given to me by my pastor's wife. I was skeptical that it would help, so I didn't write much the first few days I had it. Just a line or two, nothing positive for sure. One day after a sermon at church really challenged me, I sat down with pen and paper and decided I was going to find something good to write about. I figured it would be impossible; but pretty soon, I'd listed not one thing but three. That felt pretty good, so the next day I tried to beat my record. That time I came up*

*with five, a real victory. As you can imagine, at some point I stopped being able to one-up my blessings record; but God never has stopped using that journal and the lesson He taught me with it. I just had to buy my third journal, and I can't wait to get started on it. It's worked so well for me that the pastor's wife has asked me to teach other ladies in her Bible study group how to do their own blessings journal.*

- **Start exercising.** Walk with your kids in the neighborhood. Use workout videos from your local library or those available through your cable or satellite TV provider. Join a fitness center. You'll have the benefit of looking and feeling better! There are all sorts of scientific reasons for how the physical bolsters the emotional, but suffice it to say that God wants us moving and using our bodies in the way He designed them. Caring for ourselves on the outside will always show up on the inside, and vice versa. And it sets a wonderful example of healthy living for your children.

One of the fun things about the position you're in is that you get to figure out who you are now. . .on your own. "We" is now "Jesus and me." Perhaps you will agree with Nancy:

*I knew I wasn't alone because immediately God stepped in and started providing for my needs. It was me and God before it was me and my husband. Contrary to my current situation, God didn't leave me.*

And He hasn't left you either.

So, who are you in Jesus? What does He say? Perhaps you can begin to answer that "I wonder what I'll be when I grow up" question. When you've spent many years in a duo, you often lose a little of yourself in the process. Why not discover a few things . . .about you!

## ◯ EMBRACE IT

Congratulations! You have faced your feelings of aloneness and discovered several new things about yourself in the process.

God desires two things of you in your alone times: to draw near to Him so that He can adequately heal you, and to grow, grow, grow! Your most adventurous days are ahead, and they will be filled with great (wonderful, frightening, adventurous, blissful) things! Just hang tight with Him—and with godly friends—and you will find this learning curve is actually a gift. After all, God wants to woo you to Himself; and you're in just the right place to really connect with Him.

As we end this chapter on aloneness, take a look at Paula's story. It might surprise you.

*My husband and I were married for thirty-four years. I'd closed my eyes to his unfaithfulness time and time again. Though I hated his actions, I still didn't want him to leave because I didn't know what I'd do without him. How would I survive?*

*On the day he told me he planned to file for divorce, I panicked. For thirty-four years, I had never done anything alone. I'd leaned on him for pretty much everything. But, what choice did I have? When I moved into my new home, I was terrified. I became a recluse, afraid to go out or do much of anything. My ex-husband offered sufficient financial support, so I didn't have to look for work; but I might have been in better shape if I had. My loneliness, at times anyway, was self-induced. I convinced myself no one would want to be my friend. And I knew no one would ever want to marry me. Still, I missed being loved. I missed sharing my life with someone.*

*I remember throwing myself on my bed, beating the pillow with tears streaming down my face, and telling God that if He intended for me to be alone, then He was going to have to make me content with it. Funny thing. . .He did. He eventually convinced me that He loved me and He was with me every day, every hour, every second. Ultimately, I just needed to share my life with Him. Eventually I was able to get plugged in at my church and meet other women who'd walked a mile in my shoes. They, too, helped me see that I am never alone.*

Isn't that an amazing ending to what started as a twisted tale? God truly took Paula's pain and turned it around. Best of all, He convinced her—through His people—that she was not alone. Her relationship with the Lord was strengthened, and so was her relationship with her sisters in the Lord. The same will be true in

your case, if you just trust God to see you through this season.
Before you move on to the next section of the book, spend some
time looking at the following scriptures. Print them and tape
them up around your house. Put them in places where you'll be
confronted with them every day. On your bathroom mirror. On
the refrigerator door. On the inside of your front door. On the
dashboard of your car. Or in a prominent place on your desk at
work. There are dozens of creative places you might put them.
Memorize as many as you can. They are the tools God has given you
to overcome any feelings of aloneness you might be struggling with.

- *And when he had sent the multitudes away, he went up into
  a mountain apart to pray: and when the evening was come,
  he was there alone.*
  MATTHEW 14:23 KJV

- *God has said, "Never will I leave you; never will I forsake
  you." So we say with confidence, "The Lord is my helper;
  I will not be afraid. What can man do to me?"*
  HEBREWS 13:5–6 NIV

- *Persecuted, but not forsaken; cast down, but not destroyed.*
  2 CORINTHIANS 4:9 KJV

- *For thou art my rock and my fortress; therefore for thy name's
  sake lead me, and guide me.*
  PSALM 31:3 KJV

One final word, daughter of God: Don't look back. There's no changing the past, and the enemy will want to use it to get a foothold in territory that belongs completely to God. Replaying bad memories serves only to draw you into a place of unhappiness and, possibly, of fear; and sifting through the thoughts to find the good memories may make you long for them—and your ex—to return. What's done is done. "It is what it is," and you, daughter of the King, are standing tall and moving toward your future with your past solidly and permanently behind you.

When you're tempted to glance over your shoulder, think of how well that worked out for Lot's wife. Indeed, it's better to stumble forward than to be frozen in time with your face of salt pointing the wrong way. Rather, follow the advice of Paul, who said: "Brethren, I do not regard myself as having laid hold of it yet; but one thing I do: forgetting what lies behind and reaching forward to what lies ahead, I press on toward the goal for the prize of the upward call of God in Christ Jesus" (Philippians 3:13–14 NASB).

# Chapter 2

## *The Shock Period*

*Divorce is the psychological equivalent of a triple coronary bypass.*
*After such a monumental assault on the heart,*
*it takes years to amend all the habits and attitudes that led up to it.*
MARY KAY BLAKELY

## FACE IT

*"I'm divorced."*

What happens when you speak those words? Do you shake your head in awe, wondering how you got here? Are you still reeling that so much has happened. . .so fast? Feel like you've slipped off into a parallel universe, perhaps?

If you're like most women, you entered a period of shock once the decision to divorce was made. Perhaps you're still there. You might feel as if you're in a fog much of the time. This "Where am I?" period is really as difficult as the quote on page 37 suggests. There's no easy or fast way to process a major life change, after all. These things take time. And often, during the transition from Mrs. to Ms., time does *not* want to play nice. In fact, time may become something you rarely take note of outside of trying to keep the usual order of your day in check. Sometimes days and weeks will go by with nothing to recall except the blurriest of memories.

Rest assured this is normal given the shift in your world. During the shock period, women usually wander around in a bit of a haze, asking questions like, "Me? Divorced?" and "How did I get here?" They analyze, re-analyze, play, and replay conversations and arguments in their head, finally coming to the conclusion that nothing about this makes sense. (Truthfully, not much about divorce *does* make sense, especially during the early months.) And if you're like most Christian women, you'll also find yourself asking hard questions, like, "God, are You still there?" or "What did I ever do to deserve this?" or even "Do You still love me now that I'm divorced?"

Maybe you won't even know what to ask, because the fog is so thick. Even if you initiated the separation or divorce, you're probably still questioning what led you to such an unpredictable outcome when all you ever really wanted was what every girl wants. . .a happily-ever-after.

You might be questioning your ability to make good decisions or even be spending more time than you should in trying to avoid making new choices. Nothing makes sense. You can reason things out all day but often come up shaking your head at the end, still confused. Foggy days. Foggy thinking. Foggy mess.

Often this shock period is a season when a woman wants to hide rather than interact with people. While this, too, is normal, don't let the hiding take you away from the good things that remain in your world. Friends, family, and especially the Lord all remain and will be there for you. If you remember nothing else during this part of the grieving process, know that even if you have no one, God *never* leaves. And because He's right there (literally), He not only knows that you're in a shock period, He has the answers.

Remember Cindy, from the Introduction (pages 9–13)? When she entered the shock period, the fog overwhelmed her. She forgot to take care of little things. . .like paying the bills. Or washing clothes. Or maintaining relationships with friends and family members. Some days she would fall into bed before realizing she'd gone without a bath or even washing her face. It became necessary to make lists because a trip out of the house to run errands would often end with her car in the parking space of the grocery store or mall and no idea what she'd come for.

Cindy found herself staggering around in a blurry haze, wondering when—or if—her vision would return. Or if she even cared. Some days she found it difficult to get going in the morning. And the evenings? Well, her bed felt like the perfect place to hide away from the cares of the world. Who cared that it was only eight o'clock? Other times, she feared the pillow because of the dreams. Or the nightmares. Or, worse, the empty side of the bed.

In the midst of this craziness, Cindy found herself starting things, but not finishing them. For example, she would heat water for tea, then forget to make it. She would thaw food for supper and forget to eat it. She would finally make it to the grocery store, but not remember why she'd come. In short, her concentration skills flew out of the window.

If you're like Cindy, you're wondering when you'll return from this strange new place you've just slipped into, when your 20/20 vision will once again be intact. And though you do your best to keep putting one foot in front of the other, you find yourself questioning the very ground beneath you. Is it going to crumble? Seems the most likely scenario, all things considered. After all, your forever-marriage did exactly that.

During this volatile time, it's possible you'll forget to take care of yourself—to eat right, exercise, or go to the doctor when the need arises. You could be too stymied to keep it all clear in your head. In fact, you might be staring at a mountain of problems and issues, unable to tackle even one because you're so overwhelmed. And the advice you're receiving from well-meaning friends and family members? None of it makes much sense right now, does it? In fact, every suggestion seems impossible. . .from a psychological standpoint, anyway. You wonder if you will ever be able to function again, let alone have the kind of joy you once knew in the past.

Shock is natural. It comes with the territory, and you really can't control it. But you can be sure that it—like all things good or bad—will pass. This is just a season. Sure, you're wondering what happened to "normal," and you're probably willing to do just about anything you can think of to get things back to the way they were (with, perhaps, a few exceptions). Maybe you're even in denial. Many women in the first stages of separation and divorce don't see it for what it is. No point in denying that you're in a state of shock. It's okay to admit you don't have a handle on the usual areas of your life (the everyday stuff) right now. Shock affects the whole body—the physical, mental, emotional, and spiritual. It can cause you to freeze in place, to imagine you're dreaming. . .that you'll soon wake up, if you just pinch yourself.

Consider these words by author Brad Lewis, from his article, "Healing the Wounds of Divorce":

> *Denial. Pretending the divorce never happened or down-playing its importance. While "denial" sounds bad, it's much like physical shock after an accident: The body shuts down until it can better deal with the pain. At this stage, you may need individual counseling with a minister or a professional counselor. Counseling can help you come to terms with the*

*pain step-by-step as the initial shock of the divorce wears off.* [1]

If you're stuck in the fog, it's important to know you're not the only one who ever stumbled into this strange and unknown place. Countless Bible heroines went through seasons of shock and disbelief. Think of Abigail, whose husband committed an unpardonable act against the king. And what about Jochebed, who was forced to put her baby, Moses, into a basket in the river to save his life? Yes, these and millions of other women since have been in the very spot you're now in. They would be the first to tell you: Grieving the loss of a relationship is tough, especially in the first few weeks and months. You need to give yourself time and space. Recovery won't come overnight, but it will come. The fog will lift. The runway will clear. And then, dear sister, you will fly to heights yet unseen!

> *It's not easy taking my problems one at a time when they refuse to get in line.*
> ASHLEIGH BRILLIANT

---

[1] www.troubledwith.com/Relationships/A000000834.cfm?topic=relationships%3A%20 divorce

# GRACE IT

When you're going through the shock period, you need to give yourself permission *not* to have it all together. If you were in the middle of a horrific hurricane or tornado, would you expect to have all of your ducks in a row? A divorce is the spiritual equivalent of a catastrophic storm. You need to go easy on yourself, especially in the first weeks and months.

If you're the sort of person who has always had to put forth an image of perfection, it's time to let that go. Get rid of it. During the shock period, you need to get real with yourself. Make lists if you need to. Set up an accountability system with a friend and stick to it, even if that accountability is only to be sure you get out of bed and have a daily bath and meals. Maybe you need to find your Bible again. Do that. Don't skip reading the Word just because you can't feel the presence of God as you once did. He's there in the pages, but also within reach of your outstretched hand.

No matter what the need, be it mental or physical, you must not be too hard on yourself if you fail to meet your former standards. Grace yourself. After all, that's what God does. He extends His grace. . .freely and fully, even when we don't deserve it. *Especially* when we don't deserve it.

And even if you were able to discern whether you'd pleased God—and in this state, you may or may not have that ability— you still need to seek His face. A moment with Him can bring more clarity than any list or accountability partner.

Spend a few moments telling Him how you feel. Perhaps

you don't have the words in the moment. Rest assured, God knows your heart. He hears even before you speak, and He listens even when what you're saying may make no sense.

Perhaps you prefer to have something prepared for when the prayer need arises. Go to the Psalms and seek out passages from David's pen. The Bible is full of words of hope, of prayers that avail much. When words fail, try remembering your favorite hymn or praise chorus. Perhaps there's a song that you can reach back into your childhood and find. Sometimes those words you sang as a young girl can sound fresh and soothe your tired soul. Making a joyful noise to the Lord might be just the thing for lifting the fog, even if it's only for a moment.

Don't have a place where you feel free to sing? Of course you do. Get into the shower, turn on the water, and let loose. Not only will you be praising the Lord through the fog, but you will also be checking that box on your list where you promised to bathe.

Perhaps you're not a singer. Or maybe you would like something to print off and keep in your purse or in your drawer at work. Maybe you just need a little nudge in knowing what to say given your stunned state. If the prayer below fits your situation, offer it up to the Lord, and then watch as He lavishes His grace on you. You can read it silently, speak the words aloud, or sing them to your favorite tune while the water runs. Whatever works to reopen the communication between you and the Lord, do it.

*God, I feel like I'm wandering around in a fog. Sometimes I don't have a clue what I'm doing or how I got here, and that scares me. Things are spinning out of control, and I can't seem to get a handle on them. I never planned to be single at this point in my life, and I'm overwhelmed thinking about it. When I think about the decisions ahead, I panic. It's all just too much at times. I need You, Lord. Desperately.*

*Father, thank You that Your grace is sufficient for me. I accept it. If I ever needed it, it's now. I ask that You help me extend grace—to those who have wronged me and even to myself. Help me give myself permission to take the time to get through this without feeling like I have to make everything perfect. Lord, I submit to Your timetable and give myself over to Your amazing grace. Amen.*

## ERASE IT

*Disenchantment, whether it is a minor disappointment or a major shock, is the signal that things are moving into transition in our lives.*
WILLIAM BRIDGES

What a relief. . .to realize you don't have to have all of the answers during the shock period. And how amazing to realize that God's vision is far beyond 20/20. When you can't see what's coming around the bend, He can. And when the mountain of problems is overwhelming, He knows just which situation to handle first.

This is important because during the fog period, you might see even the smallest task as an insurmountable obstacle. Depending on the day, this might range from getting out of bed to choosing when to sell the house or change jobs. If you have children, you may be called on to mediate or even to fill the void left by the absence of their father. In whatever capacity you're needed, allow yourself the grace to know you're doing the best you can; and, when you're in the deepest moments of the fog, reach out and grasp the hand of the One who can lead you out of it. Do this even if you don't feel His presence, for He's there all the same.

Above all, however, remember you must slow down when there is fog, whether you are driving or navigating the after-effects of a divorce. It is so important that you take the time you need to get through this season of your life. You're not in a relay race. There's no one standing with a stopwatch in hand, rushing you onward. No, it's better to move at a slow, steady pace, to allow the Lord the time He needs to deal with the deep issues you're facing.

Who but the Maker can take His child from wandering to purpose again? When Jesus needed to connect with the Father, He stole away to be alone with Him. Use this fog—this period of wandering—to steal away. Let Him hold you until the strongest of the feelings subside and the fog parts, even if that's just for a moment. For just beyond the fog, the sun always returns.

If you've ever flown during a rainstorm, you will understand this. Perhaps you've fought the traffic on rain-slicked streets only to arrive at the airport and find you must slog your way through puddles in the parking lot, luggage in tow. Once at the gate, your plane is delayed due to the storm outside so you wait and wait and mull over things as you watch the dark weather. Perhaps you suffer through a stormy take-off with white knuckles, praying the clouds will part. And then they do. Somewhere between "fasten your seatbelts" and "we're now at our cruising altitude" comes a moment when the clouds fall behind and brilliant blue skies and sunshine suddenly appear.

Dear sister, we cannot promise the fog will lift like those clouds in one quick instant. Even on a short flight, there is sometimes turbulence. If the ride gets bumpy, use the time to sit, to rest, and to pray.

Think of this season of your life as you would any recovery period. You wouldn't go through open-heart surgery and then jump right back into work, would you? And you wouldn't break your leg, then jump right back into a marathon. No, healing takes time. The shock period—strange and frightening as it might feel—actually gives you time to catch your breath and draw close to God. Once there, He can begin to reveal some of the deeper issues that need His attention.

So, what are you struggling with? Go ahead. . .admit it! As you look over the following list, ask the Lord to show you the areas where you're most vulnerable during this foggy season. Then ask Him to do the work that only He can do in those areas.

Things you might be struggling with:

- Loss of control (over external circumstances and/or inner emotions)
- The inability to care for yourself (proper foods, exercise,

healthcare, hygiene)
- Weight loss or gain (from not eating enough or overeating)
- Lack of sleep (due to fear, anxiety, or excessive working)
- Loss of communication with friends and family
- Forgetting to pay bills
- Behavior or schoolwork issues with children
- Overlooking everyday tasks
- Becoming overwhelmed by the divorce proceedings and/ or the dividing of assets
- Abandonment issues that have affected your relationship with the Lord
- Fear
- Denial
- Having to make decisions on your own
- Medical issues that may have cropped up or worsened due to the stress
- Refusal to change (You just want to keep living like you lived before.)
- Redefining "normal" (You want things to be normal again.)

This is by no means a comprehensive list. Rather, the issues are as varied and unique as the readers of this book. A woman with little ones will have a different set of concerns than one who has teens or adult children. If you've never had a child, you may be mourning that lack more deeply at this point as well. Whatever the cause—and it may be too early to define some of the reasons—know there is life after this walk, but there's no way around this. You must put one foot in front of the other and walk through it.

How, you might wonder, can you go forward when what you're feeling is akin to paralysis? You can because you must. No one can remain in the fog indefinitely. The Lord won't allow it. Eventually issues will come to light and you will be forced to confront them. Perhaps you are facing that now. Sure, issues will continue to bubble forth. But refuse to allow them to overwhelm you.

It's easy to get bogged down in trying to deal with every-thing at once, so use caution. As you pray about the areas of your life where you're most vulnerable during the shock period, ask the Lord to give you clarity. . .one issue at a time. Rome wasn't built in a day, and you can't tackle the whole mountain at once. But you can handle one problem a day, fog or no fog. Make up your mind to do it, and God will surely walk alongside you, His supernatural fog light guiding the way.

If you are having trouble deciding which issue to address— or to ignore—perhaps a list is in order. Cindy wrote down the things that seemed to zing past her then ping-pong back again. She kept the lists in a place where she could, in God's timing, address them. Cindy kept a notepad in her purse and one in her kitchen. Not only did she write down her daily to-do list (which often meant merely repeating the one from the previous day), but she also made notes to herself to recall phone numbers, appointments, and anything else she otherwise might forget.

If you choose to go this route, don't get caught up in trying to write everything down. Just put on paper what's in your heart, then set it aside to pray over or deal with when the fog has lifted. If nothing else, you can be assured that these things won't be forgotten.

# CREPLACE IT

*An unmarried woman or virgin is concerned about the Lord's affairs: Her aim is to be devoted to the Lord in both body and spirit.*
1 CORINTHIANS 7:34 NIV

It might be tough to function during the shock period, but taking steps—even if they're baby steps—is critical to your survival. With God's help, you can and will learn that you're capable of doing great things. . .even when you don't feel like it. *Especially* when you don't feel like it.

So, where do you begin? How can you turn fog into a runway for success? By staying alert and committing to work hard, even when the task seems impossible.

Instead of moaning, "I have to make *all* of these decisions on my own!" change your thinking. What a blessing. . .you *get* to make choices for yourself. Maybe there are dreams you tucked away that you can pull out and dust off. If you've forgotten, ask the Lord to remind you of the things you may have set aside during your marriage. But don't get stuck in the future, either. Even the everyday things—like housing questions, paperwork, bills, and so forth, can be adventurous, if you make up your mind to approach them as such.

So, lift that chin! There's work to be done. And shock or no shock, fog or no fog, you can do it. . .with God's help.

- **When struggling with feelings of denial, ask God for courage.** Yes, facing the truth can be a challenge, but it's the healthiest way to move forward. Hiding from the truth will only prolong your hurting. The Lord will undergird you with His strength, and you'll be able to see the truth for what it is—no more and no less.

- **When you feel as if you've lost control over external circumstances and/or internal emotions, remind yourself that you were never in control anyway.** God holds the reins. And if you're the sort of person who longs to fix things (circumstances or people), this might be a good time to confess that and ask the Lord to help you take your hands off so that He can move on your behalf.

- **If you're struggling to care for yourself (to eat proper foods, exercise, get adequate healthcare, or even perform basic hygiene functions), make up your mind to do it, whether you feel like it or not.** Get dressed. Take a walk. Continue with your vitamin and medication regimen. Doing these things will help give you clarity. So will eating right. A poor diet leads to foggy thinking. So, if you handle this one area first, all of the other areas will be easier to tackle.

- **Get enough sleep.** It's a simple sentiment, and yet even the average woman does not do it. A minimum of seven hours of sleep is a must, especially in times such as these. Your body is under physical demands, and only the re-charging time spent with your head on the pillow will fend off the exhaustion that accompanies such a loss. Sleep deprivation can worsen your ability to think, cause you to be unable to make competent decisions, and even manifest itself in physical issues that will send you to the doctor's office. Perhaps you are finding sleep difficult. There are any number of tricks to finding rest, from the tried and true warm bath and hot milk to a good book and a new set of pillows and sheets. Perhaps your situation requires more. A frank discussion with your doctor may be in order. In any case, do what you can to protect those hours of rest. It is essential for your recovery.

- **Loss of communication with friends and family.** Pick a person a day to communicate with (be it a family member or good friend), even if you don't feel like speaking to a soul. Make a point to not grow distant. Yes, this will be a tough one, especially if isolation feels more comfortable. Of course, you don't want to answer questions or tell someone for the hundredth time you're fine. These are things you've probably done over and over until you can't remember any other topic to discuss. But, dear sister in Christ, if you go too long without communicating with others, feelings of aloneness will creep back in, and that will only complicate things further. It will also give you too much time to think and not enough time to do the healing work that is necessary to leave the fog behind. If you don't feel up to phone calls at first, then try text messages or e-mails. But only for a season, as it is essential to keep in face-to-face contact with those who love you.

- **Weight loss or gain.** Women handle stress in different ways. Some turn to food, others turn away from it.

Don't overlook meals, even if the food holds no appeal. You need the nourishment. But don't turn to food for comfort, either. Every time you're tempted to do so, turn to the Word instead. If you're struggling with weight gain, consider joining a group like First Place or Weight Watchers. There, you will find the support you need. You may also make a much-needed friend or two. In addition, the process of getting control over this one area of your life—your food intake and exercise—can be a healthy step forward. Not only does this choice mean you are moving forward toward a better life, but it also has physical benefits beyond weight loss. Nutrition is key, and exercise causes endorphins to release, giving you a sense of accomplishment and giving you a natural emotional boost.

- **Forgetting to pay bills.** Make a certain day of the month bill paying day. It might be a tough day, but if you're prepared for it—physically and psychologically— things will go much smoother. If you're too wrapped up in the fog, ask for help from a trusted friend. Between the two of you, create a workable plan. Then ask that friend to come over once a month to help you implement the plan. Perhaps you could have someone set up your bill paying online so that the process is streamlined. Many banks offer this service. When faced with the click of a mouse rather than the writing of multiple checks, the process may seem much more manageable to you.

- **Overlooking everyday tasks.** As you're able, make a to-do list. It's easy to overlook things if you're not paying attention. Making a list (and putting it on your fridge) will help remind you to do little things. Or do as mentioned previously and keep a pad of paper near you not just to take note of additions to your list but also to keep track of other things you'd otherwise forget. As with bill paying, perhaps you can find a friend to keep you accountable or even designate a certain day of the week for particular tasks.

- **You're overwhelmed by divorce proceedings/dividing of assets.** Look for help from an attorney or friend who has walked this road ahead of you. If you are unable to afford an attorney, try looking into free legal assistance in your community. Or go to your home church and inquire as to any references they might be able to offer. You might be surprised to learn that there are people with expertise who want to help, even if you can't afford to pay.

- **Abandonment issues have affected your relationship with the Lord.** It's time to get to the heart of any abandonment issues you might have, but don't rush yourself through this process. Your heavenly Father wants you to know that He will never leave you or abandon you. The next few weeks and months will prove that. There are good Bible studies out there to address this topic, but you may not be ready to work through them just yet. Know, however, that until you can do the digging needed to find what God says about this, you should be able to rest in the knowledge that He will not leave you.

- **Fear.** Memorize fear-combative scriptures. Then, every time you're afraid, those words will spring to mind. If left unchecked, fear can immobilize you. Worse, it can cause the entire process of healing from your divorce to come to a standstill. And the devil would love nothing better than for you to stay right where you are: in a fog-induced coma where he can keep you as a captive audience to his lies. Resist and flee, for fear is not your friend, nor should it be embraced as a way to live.

- **Finally, having to make decisions on your own can be a challenge, particularly if you're accustomed to having someone to bounce your ideas off of.** Ask a good friend or family member to take this role temporarily, or even a trusted counselor at church. Seeking wise counsel is invaluable at this time, even if you feel you're doing fine in this area. Often the decisions we make during the fog period are ones we regret later. Consider Annie's story:

> *When my husband and I put together the paperwork for our divorce, I had the option of either receiving half of his retirement monies and half of the proceeds from the house, or keeping the house and forfeiting all retirement monies. I went with keeping the house, because I was frozen in place and didn't know what else to do. (We did a do-it-yourself-*

*divorce, no attorneys involved.) In retrospect, I wish I'd opted to do the half and half thing. Staying in the house proved to be somewhat traumatic. Too many memories. If I could do it all over again, I'd use the "take the money and run" philosophy. These kinds of things are why you need an attorney or a counselor to guide you. I wish I'd had one.*

It's time to move out of the fog, sister! Leave the past in the past. Sure, you don't feel like it. Your world has been upended and nothing is where it once was. The sooner you learn to leave the past where it belongs, the sooner you will begin moving out of the haze. And dealing with things head-on is the only way to move forward. Otherwise, you will remain stagnant and eventually give in to your fears and negative emotions. No, you might not move at breakneck speed, but you will make progress. So, up and at 'em, girl!

## ⊂EMBRACE IT

The shock period can be a tough time, but it's the best time for a shift in attitude. The Lord is going to use this time to work out some things in your life, and He's also going to use it to springboard you into a terrific future. . .if you let Him. So, hang on for the ride! Don't let this season hold you back. There's plenty of joy ahead for a tenacious woman like you!

Don't believe it? Well, the Bible promises there will be joy in the morning. Before the morning can come, however, you must make your way through the darkness. You can, and will, with His guidance. Reach out. He's there. Don't feel Him? He's still there.

As we close out this section on the shock period, take a look at Beth's story. You may be able to relate.

*My husband and I had twenty-five wonderful years together. He was the perfect husband and father and an awesome Sunday school teacher at our church. The children in his class adored him. So did the guys on the church softball team. He was everyone's picture of the perfect guy. Every day I thanked God for giving me a life that others only dreamed of. We couldn't have been happier. Or so I thought.*

*The news that my husband wanted a divorce came from out of left field. I honestly didn't believe it when I heard it. Nothing made any sense, especially the part where he informed me that he would be moving thousands of miles away to be with the woman he'd fallen in love with. My body literally went into shock. Over the next few weeks, I lost a considerable amount of weight and (due to the shock) went into menopause several years ahead of time. I was unable to eat and wondered how I could ever survive. I had to become both mother and father to our four children, though at times I could barely push the covers back on the bed.*

*The whole thing felt like a terrible nightmare. I kept wishing I would wake up. Only the Lord got me through that season. If not for Him, I never would have made it.*

*Over time, the fog began to lift. I couldn't see the road ahead with much clarity, but I began to take steps in faith. With every step I took, I gained confidence not in myself, but in my Savior, who promised to lead me through this season in His power, not my own. Sometimes I think the Lord protected me in the fog. He sent it as a buffer, to shield me from some of the pain. While I wouldn't want to go back and experience any of that initial pain again, I do sometimes miss God's natural "anesthesia" that went along with it.*

God moved in Beth's life during the shock period, and He will move in yours as well. While you're walking through this season, take advantage of the words of life offered to you in the Bible. Here are some great verses to memorize to bring you hope:

- *From the ends of the earth I call to you, I call as my heart grows faint; lead me to the rock that is higher than I.*
  PSALM 61:2 NIV

- *But you are a shield around me, O LORD; you bestow glory on me and lift up my head.*
  PSALM 3:3 NIV

- *My shield is God Most High, who saves the upright in heart.*
  PSALM 7:10 NIV

- *With your help I can advance against a troop; with my God I can scale a wall.*
  PSALM 18:29 NIV

- *Why are you downcast, O my soul? Why so disturbed within me? Put your hope in God, for I will yet praise him, my Savior and my God.*
  PSALM 42:11 NIV

As stunned as you might have been when your marriage ended, God was not. His vision is far superior, and He knows how to navigate you through this shock period. Spend some time with the scriptures listed above, and watch how God works. And while you're at it, consider the following quote:

*"Success is never wondering what-if."*
KARRIE HUFFMAN

# Chapter 3

# *Oh, Those Changes!*

*When we are no longer able to change a situation,*
*we are challenged to change ourselves.*
VICTOR FRANKL

# ⟳ FACE IT

If you've walked through a separation or divorce, then you know what it's like to go through a lifetime of changes in a short period of time. Sometimes it can feel like you've pressed the FAST-FORWARD button on the DVR. Things begin to move so quickly you can't see them in perspective. They go whirring by and you sit, a spectator. If you're like most women, you often wish you had a remote control so that you could press the PAUSE button.

Think of all the shifts you've endured. It's likely you've had a change of attitude and maybe even a change in living arrangement and lifestyle. It's likely you've had to change your perceptions and some of your relationships. And what about changes in activity level? Family dynamics? Schedules? You've certainly also been through major shifts in your thinking and your heart.

Even if you're an adventurous soul, the sudden shifts might be a bit daunting. Just about the time you think you have a handle on something, *bam!* Another shift.

Yes, change is inevitable. But it's certainly not all bad. Most of our "life shifts" are uncomfortable, but result in stronger, happier days ahead. Sure, you might be going through some negative changes right now (at least, as you perceive them), but there are plenty of positive ones, too. You might have to search a little harder to find them, but they're there! For example, there's that new mindset, the one that whispers, "I'm free to be who I really want to be!" in your ear.

How we deal with change is critical to our survival. If we

fight it, resist it, approach it with balled-up fists, then we will live discontented lives on the other side of it—and that is never good. But if we welcome it, invite it, move forward with peace in our hearts, then we have the added benefit of changing not just the external things, but internal as well. After all, what good would it do you to go through changes on the outside if you weren't willing to make a few adjustments on the inside, too?

Yes, of course it's the external that seems the easiest. Scrub the skin and it glows. Sear the soul, and there isn't a whole lot that's visible. But God sees, and He knows. And He wants to use this season to bring about the greatest change of all: healing in your heart.

Because life is in an ever-changing state, you need to stay flexible, especially now! And you're in good company! Countless women of God have experienced major life shifts. Consider Naomi, who lost her husband and made the monumental decision to travel back to her homeland. Think about Deborah, a woman who had such a strong calling on her life that she stepped outside of her comfort zone to fulfill it. Consider Esther, who left one lifestyle (as a simple Jewish girl) to become a queen. All of these women experienced major transformations in their lives, and all came out better for it in the end. The same is true in your case. Don't resist the shifts. They're going to move you to a place of wholeness and strength. Let God have His way in the changes, and He may surprise you with the outcome!

Cindy went through multiple changes in her life—several of them on top of each other. In fact, things were changing so rapidly that she almost lost her footing. She didn't feel grounded.

Maybe you can relate to that.

After divorcing, Cindy and her ex-husband were forced to sell the home they had lived in for over fifteen years. In that moment—as the deed to the property changed hands—years of memories flashed before her eyes. The pain was unbearable. How could she leave the place where her children had grown up? Where she and her husband had hosted Sunday school parties and anniversary celebrations? Where she'd baked birthday cakes and Christmas pies? Even the awful color her husband painted their daughter's room—a color chosen to please a six-year-old and not her mother—looked good as the movers arrived.

Cindy didn't want to make the change to a new place. It seemed impossible to her. Overwhelming, even. Packing. Lifting. Lugging. Deciding what should stay and what should go. How could she handle that? And to move to such a small place after living in a big house? Impossible! Where would she put the big dining room table—the one where countless Christmas dinners had been served? It certainly wouldn't fit in her new home. Not that she wanted to call it home, anyway. No, it was just a place—an unfamiliar, scary place—where her furniture and unpacked boxes now resided. And besides, there was one less place setting needed at that table anyway, so why bother?

Yes, Cindy had a tough time with change. But she eventually made the move. . .kicking and screaming all the way. She changed her address. Changed her checking account number. Changed her utilities. Changed her daily routine. Changed her living standards. Changed her hairstyle and the place where she shopped for groceries. Changed the way she communicated with her ex-in-laws and other extended family members. Changed the music she listened to. (Who wants to listen to love songs when you're separated?) Changed the last thing she said at night before going to sleep. She even gave thought to changing churches. And it all seemed to be happening at warp speed. Her friends put on their most encouraging smiles and called it an adventure. Cindy, however, called it a whirlwind—a tornado that lifted her out of her comfortable life and deposited her in the midst of an unfamiliar place with no idea how she got there.

Do you feel Cindy's pain? Have you walked a mile in her shoes? If so, then you already know that change is a necessary part of the journey. To get from one place to another, you have to take steps, and taking steps always requires adjustment. Instead of balking at the shifts in your life, take a deep breath and ask God to help you with your determination. He will do it. Before you know it, you'll be as flexible as a gymnast.

Hard to imagine? You can do it, sister! But you have to take one step at a time. Even an Olympian must start with a stretch before tackling anything. Begin at the beginning (a very good place to start!), and you will soon see the path begin to clear and the way become more open. It will take time to adapt to these changes, and there is no right or wrong way to learn what is best for you.

Here's what Christian therapist, Beverly Blackstone, has to say about change:

*The one thing we know about life is that change is a constant. That's not a conundrum; it's a fact. When things are very good, they'll change; and when things are very bad, they'll change.*

*No one gets married thinking it will end badly. As my covenant marriage died, I remember the ominous feeling of the body bag zipping shut on my love, significance, and security. When my husband changed his "I do" to "I don't," my status changed from "chosen" to the scarlet "D." Nineteen years were flushed away, and my future was bleak. I was desperate and needy and felt like I'd never be okay again. My marriage was supposed to supply my basic needs, and now, in the midst of too many changes, I had to change my supplier.*

*Desperation drove me back to my other covenant, the one with someone who is not a man who lies (Numbers 23:19). Someone who promises lifetime love (Jeremiah 31:3). Someone who feels my pain (Hebrews 4:15). Someone who will supply all my needs (Philippians 4:19). Someone who lets me sleep peacefully in the safety of His security (Psalm 4:8). This covenant-keeper, Jesus, has met all my needs, and is a change that just keeps changing for the better.*

Today, as you contemplate the many changes in your life, don't look at them as bad things. Think of them as changes for the better—motions that will take you toward the new life God has for you. In fact, that's exactly what they are.

# GRACE IT

So, you're facing multiple changes, and you're stumped. You don't know how to handle them. Don't be too hard on yourself. God knows right where you are and is giving you the grace you need to walk through this season. . .even now. Consider this verse from 1 Corinthians 1:4 (kjv): "I thank my God always on your behalf, for the grace of God which is given you by Jesus Christ."

Are you struggling with being thankful for the changes you're enduring? God wants you to trust Him and be thankful He is trustworthy. There will come a day when the changes will be behind you and a future that is much clearer will lie ahead. Until then, lean on His grace. And where does that grace come from? Jesus Christ, of course. He is the giver of grace.

Think about that. He came to this earth and walked through a host of challenges, far greater than any we will ever know. He understands the need for grace as we go through major shifts in our lives, and stands with hand extended to offer it freely as you put one foot in front of the other. He offers not just grace to be saved, mind you, but grace to go through every change you will ever face. Why not spend a little time chatting with Him about that?

*Lord, I have to admit, I haven't always reached out and grabbed hold of Your grace. There may have been times I didn't even want it. Or perhaps I couldn't recognize it for all the worries I let cloud my vision. Today, I thank You for extending grace for these changes I'm going through. Help me to "grace" myself through this process, too, Lord. With*

*every new change, may I remember that I don't have to
have it all together. I ask for Your direction, Lord. Protect
me as my life takes a few strange twists and turns. Walk me
through these many, many changes. Amen.*

## ⟡ ERASE IT

> *Every evening I turn my worries over to God.*
> *He's going to be up all night anyway.*
> MARY C. CROWLE

Some of the changes you're going through will frustrate you;
others you will welcome. Some make you angry; others bring a
sense of relief. In order to erase any angst you might be feeling
over the changes you're facing, it's good to know what you're
dealing with.

Look over the following list of things that might have
changed in your life, and see if you can identify with any of
them.

What has changed since your separation/divorce?

- Your attitude
- How people look at you (or how you think they look at
  you)
- How you look at men
- Your responsibilities

- Your income
- How you view permanence/long-lasting relationships
- Your schedule (work and/or home)
- How you deal with the kids
- Your housing situation
- Your church or Sunday school situation
- Your social life
- How you shop/cook
- Your interests
- What you do with the kids
- Holidays
- The television shows/movies you watch
- Bedtime rituals
- Your weight or physical appearance
- Your job situation
- Your beneficiaries
- Your name
- Your clothing/hairdo
- The music you listen to

As you look over the list, see the changes for what they are. Which ones really bug you? Which ones are welcome changes? If the negative changes outweigh the positive ones, why not take the time to tweak the bad ones in your favor? Turn those negative changes into positives.

Begin to see these things in perspective. Many of these changes are, after all, good ones. As for the ones you're struggling with, decide to make one more change: Change your mind.

Decide once and for all that you are capable of doing whatever it takes to come out stronger on the other side of this.

## C REPLACE IT

So, life feels a bit like a revolving door. Still, who says change has to be a bad thing? Think about it. From the time you were a little girl, you've faced changes. Stepping onto the school bus for the first time. Starting your period. Changes in your physical appearance in junior high and high school. Changes in the things you liked to eat. Developing a waistline. Changing your wardrobe. (Think of all of the different styles you've worn over the years!) Getting past those irritating pimples that accompanied the teen years. Going off to college or finding that first job. Moving out of your parents' home. Finding and marrying your husband. Learning to adjust to your role as a wife and possibly as a mother. Changing is a part of life. And the more we fight it, the harder we make things for ourselves.

The word *transform* is a synonym for change. Many women fear change because they find it difficult to move past the comfortable place where they've settled. Maybe you've resisted the changes that have been thrust upon you. You're irritated that things couldn't stay the same. (After all, they stayed the same for years and you did just fine. Right?)

It's time for a change of thinking! Time to transform your thoughts. Only then will you truly transform your life. All changes—good and bad—begin in the mind, after all. You have to make up your mind. Otherwise, you'll just be going through the motions.

The next time you're tempted to complain about all of the changes you're going through, take a look at what the Bible has to say about transformation. After all, we're called to be transformed. Changed. How? By renewing our minds. Why? So that we can "prove what is that good, and acceptable, and perfect, will of God" (Romans 12:2 KJV).

You're transforming. Morphing from a caterpillar to a butterfly. Don't fight the process, especially during the stressful times. Let it happen. You have been supernaturally gifted to get through this. Fighting the change only makes things worse. The truth is, changes will happen whether you invite them or not. By taking God's hand and allowing Him to lead you through them, you just might find yourself welcoming the woman you are becoming. But first, you have to get real and understand you're not losing who you are. Rather, you are gaining the new you. . .the one the Lord is creating even now.

Let's take another look at some of those changes you're going through, so that you can begin to see God's solutions.

- **Change in perception.** Maybe you're worried about how people are looking at you now that you're no longer married. Let's face it: women are always concerned about what others are thinking about them. Instead of worrying about others (and how they're viewing the changes you're going through), focus on what God thinks. He's holding your hand and guiding you, step-by-step. His opinion is the one that matters most. And frankly, most people aren't thinking about you at all. They're focused on themselves.

- **Changes in your income.** Are you trying to get by on less money than before? This probably isn't the first time you've been through a major shift in your finances. Were you like many women who started their married lives with a tiny checkbook balance and big plans? Perhaps you can recall that first big promotion? Or, as many women have experienced, that layoff or ending of work to stay home with children? In each case, your budget expanded or shrank based on changes. Maybe these were changes you planned or perhaps they were surprises. Pause to think about the strides you've already made. Have you ever faced financial struggles in the past? If so, who saw you through them? God hasn't changed, remember? If He saw you through those rough times in the past, He'll do it again. And again!

- **Changes in the way you view men.** This isn't the first time your view of men has changed. Think of how you viewed men as a toddler. Remember how your thinking shifted when you got to your teens? When you reached your twenties, your views on men changed again. And when things in the marriage began to shift, your view of men probably shifted right along with them. In other words, you've spent your life changing your views on men. Now you have a new perspective. Just remember that you can't lump all men into one category. If your husband broke your heart, that's no indicator that all men are heartbreakers. If your husband was the sort who wouldn't step up to the plate and take responsibility, it doesn't mean that all men are irresponsible. Take your worries about men to the Lord, and ask Him to show you the truth of how you should properly view the men in your world. Trust is essential, but earned. Let God lead you in the process.

- **Changes in responsibilities.** Maybe you were used to caring for your husband's needs above your own. Now you forget to factor him out of the equation. Old habits die hard, but new ones can replace them if you work at it. As you've aged (whether you're twenty or eighty) your responsibilities have routinely changed. You had certain responsibilities in school. Certain responsibilities as a daughter. Certain responsibilities as a mother (if you have children). Responsibilities on the job. Responsibilities in your church or community. On and on the list goes. Your responsibilities have always been in a state of flux. So. . .keep on fluxing!

- **Change of viewpoint.** Maybe you've experienced a change in how you view lifelong relationships. That's understandable. But remember, what happened in your marriage isn't an indicator of things across the board. Happily-ever-afters really do exist, both in this life and the one ahead. This is another issue of trust. Give yourself time and keep leaning into what the Lord says about relationships. Perhaps a discussion with a counselor or participation in a group study for women in your situation will help.

- **Schedule changes.** Your schedule is probably changing, but that's not necessarily a bad thing. There's one less person to accommodate, and that just might work to your advantage, time-wise. Perhaps in the past you had to accommodate your day to fit his. Now you're free to work around your own needs. Schedule changes affect many areas of your life, including meal preparation and grocery shopping. Maybe your workload will decrease, giving you more time to do the things you enjoy. Not that you can rest on your laurels! If you still have kids at home, you're almost certainly going through some changes in how you deal with them. They're going through changes, too. Be patient as their schedules and yours begin to eventually mesh. It is a process and will not be worked out overnight.

- **Beneficiary changes.** This is one thing that newly divorced women often overlook. If you have a will (and you need one), you need to make sure you pay close attention to who will receive your assets when you're gone. Most women who have grown children choose one of the kids. Others select a parent or a good friend. Still others choose to make their church (or some religious organization) the beneficiary. Regardless, this is something you'll want to take care of. But even this doesn't have to be a downer. Just take it in stride.

- **Church changes.** When it comes to your church situation, move slowly and prayerfully. Don't abruptly leave your Sunday school class or your church. It might be hard to spend time with people, especially in a couples' class, but face it. . .those are the people who probably know you best. They want to walk you through this. There may come a time when you need to shift to another class, but do so carefully, after praying about it. And don't assume that you need to change churches to get away from what you're feeling. No matter where you go, you will face the same emotions, especially if you choose a large church where no one knows you, where you don't have someone to keep an eye on you. Seek wise counsel from your pastor or accountability partners before making any decisions. When the time comes to make the move, be it from the couples' to the singles' class or from your home church to a new one, you will have made the decision with care.

- **Weight changes.** Maybe you're one of those people who has gone through a major shift in weight since your separation. Perhaps you've lost a significant amount of weight because food is no longer appealing. Or maybe you're one of those who turns to food for comfort. Understand this is a pattern that needs to be broken as there is no comfort to be found in an expanding waistline. The opposite may, in fact, happen. It's normal to see some fluctuation in weight during a major life-shift, but keep a close eye on that. You might need to visit your doctor or nutritionist so that he/she can monitor your food intake. If you're having trouble making good food choices, consider taking a multivitamin to keep up your strength.

Change is coming. It's in the air. And it's a good change, not bad. We are called to conform (change) into the image of Christ. "For whom he did foreknow, he also did predestinate to be conformed to the image of his Son, that he might be the firstborn among many brethren" (Romans 8:29 KJV). This happens on a daily basis. Little by little, we are changing to be more like Him.

And think about the ultimate change. . .when we are caught up to be with Christ for all eternity. "In a moment, in the twinkling of an eye, at the last trump: for the trumpet shall sound, and the dead shall be raised incorruptible, and we shall be changed" (1 Corinthians 15:52 KJV).

Doesn't this put things in perspective? Perhaps the things you're going through now are simply a foretaste of that which is to come. Now, that's a glorious thought! C'mon, change! Bring it on!

# ◖ EMBRACE IT

*All changes, even the most longed for, have their melancholy;*
*for what we leave behind us is a part of ourselves;*
*we must die to one life before we can enter another.*
ANATOLE FRANCE

The Bible teaches us that God never changes. He's the same yesterday, today, and forever. But we. . .His kids? Well, we're always changing! Without these alterations to our imperfect selves, how would the Lord mold us and shape us in His image? Embrace the changes, and watch God transform you—from caterpillar to magnificent butterfly!

As we close out this section on change, take a look at Connie's story:

*I went through so many changes after my marriage ended. That whole period of time was like a blur; but it's one I now look back on with a smile on my face, realizing God was right there, guiding me. My situation might have been changing, but His wasn't. He was the same God who had seen me through crises in the past and the same God who would see me through once again.*

*I was already working, so I continued down that same path, thanks to my supportive boss. I took classes at night to work on my degree and also took banking classes. My boss also gave me a raise so I didn't have to quit and take a job at the local factory for more money. He later promoted me to Assistant Manager. No females had been assigned to that job before. Talk about God's favor!*

*I could sense the Lord literally walking me through it all, every step of the way. I attended church faithfully and actively read my Bible daily, which constantly reminded me of God's love for me. Though I went through many changes, they grew me into the person I now am. I won't say it was easy. . .but it was worth it.*

Don't you love that story? Sure, Connie faced some changes when her marriage ended. But look at her adventurous spirit. No angst in that story! Instead of complaining, she allowed God to take her to new heights. But you're not like Connie, you say? How do you know until you let the Lord work in your life?

You see, your story isn't so different, really. If you're willing to be transformed inside and out, God can and will do remarkable things! Our unchanging God is the only One who can truly help us through the changes we're going through. You have the Holy Spirit—the Comforter—resident within you! Think about that for a moment. The same Comforter who whispered, "You can do this" to Shadrach, Meshach, and Abednego. The same Comforter who hovered over the Israelites as they made their trek through the desert. The same Comforter who led Esther through the process of saving her people. *That* Comforter lives in you.

Not up to the challenge yet? You will be—in the Lord's strength!

As you're going through this season of transformation,

take a look at the following scriptures. They will provide the encouragement you need.

- *To every thing there is a season, and a time to every purpose under the heaven.*
  ECCLESIASTES 3:1 KJV

- *For I am the LORD, I change not; therefore ye sons of Jacob are not consumed.*
  MALACHI 3:6 KJV

- *And be not conformed to this world: but be ye transformed by the renewing of your mind, that ye may prove what is that good, and acceptable, and perfect, will of God.*
  ROMANS 12:2 KJV

- *He hath made every thing beautiful in his time.*
  ECCLESIASTES 3:11 KJV

God does, indeed, make everything beautiful in His time. That's one thing you can count on. But in order to make things beautiful, you have to be like it to go the distance, to allow the changes to take place, whether you're willing or not.

You can trust Him, you know. In case you have any doubt about that, read the twenty-third psalm. In those well-loved verses, the Lord promises to guide you like a shepherd and to make sure you have the things you need. *(Verse 1: The LORD is my shepherd; I shall not want.)*

He promises to give you a place where you can rest and get refreshed during life's changes. *(Verse 2: He maketh me to lie down in green pastures: he leadeth me beside the still waters.)*

He promises that the changes you're going through won't break you down, and He promises to continue giving you direction for the changes ahead. *(Verse 3: He restoreth my soul: he leadeth me in the paths of righteousness for his name's sake.)*

He promises that even in the hardest of changes, the deepest of valleys, He will not only guide you but will go with you. *(Verse 4: Yea, though I walk through the valley of the shadow of death, I will fear no evil: for thou art with me; thy rod and thy staff they comfort me.)*

He promises that, through thick and thin, in the presence of friends or enemies, in the midst of the craziest changes, you can dwell with Him all of the days of your life (even the days when things are spinning out of control). Best of all, good things are coming! No doubt about it. So, look at those changes as a good thing! *(Verses 5 and 6: Thou preparest a table before me in the presence of mine enemies: thou anointest my head with oil; my cup runneth over. Surely goodness and mercy shall follow me all the days of my life: and I will dwell in the house of the LORD for ever.)*

Are you ready to allow the unchanging God of the universe to walk you through the changes ahead? If so, be prepared to watch Him grow you into a different person—someone stronger, healthier, and happier. The ultimate goal here is a fabulous life on the other side of the changes. It's waiting, sister! Just watch and see.

*Change has a considerable psychological impact on the human mind.
To the fearful it is threatening because it means that things may get
worse. To the hopeful it is encouraging because things may get better.
To the confident it is inspiring because the challenge
exists to make things better.*
KING WHITNEY JR.

# Chapter 4

## *Dealing with Fear*

*You gain strength, courage, and confidence by every experience
in which you really stop to look fear in the face. . . .
You must do the thing you think you cannot do.*
Eleanor Roosevelt

# ⟡ FACE IT

Ah, fear. That niggling feeling that grips us when we go through seasons where we feel like we've lost control. Fear often targets those who are most vulnerable: people who are already going through challenges. It sneaks in unannounced and uninvited. . . at the very moment you need to be strong. Worse, fear causes you to take your attention off what God is going to do in order to focus on what might happen. Talk about hitting below the belt!

Fear grips us in the strangest of ways, and often when we least expect it. When faced with a sudden decision. When we hear something go *bump* in the night. When we're standing in a courtroom, facing the inevitable banging of the gavel. When our month is longer than our paycheck. When we face unforeseen challenges with our children. When the car breaks down. When the phone rings and it's that nice fellow from the singles group. Fear nuzzles up next to us like a comfortable friend, then surprises us with its sting.

Maybe you're of the mindset that godly people shouldn't have to struggle with fear. Maybe you even feel unspiritual because you're wrestling with it. Instead of beating yourself up, take a look at several of the people in the Word of God who faced this same battle. What about the disciples, huddled up on the boat, facing a mighty storm? The Bible is pretty clear: They were shaking in their boots! And what about Peter? When asked about his association with Jesus, he gave a coward's response. Think of Gideon. His fear caused him to hide from his enemies. On and on the list goes. People throughout time have struggled with fear!

What are you afraid of? Might as well admit it. Are you afraid of sleeping—or *living*—alone? Scared you'll make poor choices? Afraid of change? Or are you, perhaps, fearful that things might stay the same? Many single women are afraid of the unknown, of what might—or might not—be waiting around that next bend. They're also scared they will make poor choices. Some even go so far as to question whether they should have gotten married in the first place. "If I made a poor choice by marrying the wrong person, maybe all of my choices will be bad!"

Yes, there are many things a newly single woman could be afraid of, if she were so inclined. But while these are all legitimate concerns, God doesn't want them to cripple you. He wants to walk you through these things with the faith and confidence that He is in control. . .even when it feels like everything is spinning out of control.

Take a look at what Christian psychiatrist Paul Looney has to say on the subject:

> *After divorce, anxiety and fear are completely normal. Anytime we face something new or different, the unknown arouses fear. Change is difficult, even if it is good change. When God led His people into the wilderness, they faced some fear. When He was ready to lead them into the Promised Land, their fears were even greater. Though it would be nice to think God's path would never cause fear, He plans to take us out of our comfort zone. Sometimes, divorce is a step toward trusting God in a new way.*
>
> *Naturally, much fear and anxiety comes as a direct*

*assault from the enemy. He wants to take you down, and
he always strikes when you are most vulnerable. Remember
that many of the voices in your head are not your own. He
is not called "the accuser" for nothing. When a marriage
ends, he is quick to heap blame, shame, guilt, and con-
demnation. It helps if you know who you are in Christ
and claim your identity in Him.*

*If there is a specific fear, write it down. Face it. Imagine
the scenario playing out in your mind. God does not want
you to live in fear. If you fear that something would destroy
you or your faith, God would rather you walk through
it than live the rest of your life in fear. When you walk
through your worst-case scenario on paper, you often realize
that God is perfectly prepared to see it through.*

Rest assured, fear is not from God. In fact, it's not really
even an emotion, like joy or sorrow. Fear is an enemy that needs
to be confronted. So, when you're faced with that gripping
sensation, do as Eleanor Roosevelt suggested in the quote at the
beginning of the chapter. Look it in the face. Don't shy away.
Don't let it freeze you in your tracks. Get bold! Deal with it.

How do you deal with fear? Do you grab yourself by the
bootstraps and muster up the necessary courage to keep going?
Do you pray your way through it? Do you cave in, hiding under
the covers? Women deal with fear in a variety of ways. Everyone
has to find her own way to battle it. What works for some might
not work for others.

Let's take a look at how Cindy dealt with her fear. After years of being cared for by her husband, she found herself without a covering, financially and emotionally. Unfortunately, she allowed the resulting fear to stop her from moving forward. Everything in her life came to a standstill when the fear kicked in. Why? She couldn't explain it, exactly. She just couldn't seem to function anymore. She was afraid of the changes she found herself going through. She was also afraid of things staying the same. In short, she was stuck.

Eventually she came to grips with reality. Either she could go on—knotted up with fear—or she could call a spade a spade. Cindy took a new approach. She crawled out from under the covers, rose to her feet, put her hands on her hips, and began to speak to the fear with authority. Sure, she still faced struggles. But she gave up on the notion that fear was a friend. She saw it for what it was: her mortal enemy.

And fear is just that, straight from our mortal enemy, the devil. It is his best tool to distract us and push us out of the comforting embrace of our Father in heaven. Being afraid means you're concentrating not on what God will do to get you through this trial but on what He isn't doing. Or, worse, on what may happen when He doesn't act. None of this is productive thinking, nor will it give you a basis for moving forward in faith. Rather, it puts you right where the devil wants you: in the palm of his hand.

Maybe you can relate to Cindy. Have you been through seasons where you've felt stuck in your fear? Perhaps you're still there. If you're in that tricky place, take the time to admit it. Tell the Lord you feel trapped. He already knows it anyway, but confessing it will help you find the release you need. This may be a good time to speak to a professional, such as a counselor or pastor. Sometimes this fear is indicative of resistance to the changes you need to make to move forward in your healing. Once you've admitted you've been held captive by fear, you can finally begin to take the necessary steps to find the freedom you need. And that freedom is what will help you to find healing and a bright future post-divorce. It might not happen overnight, but those tentacles of fear will release their hold. . .in Jesus' name!

*The LORD is my light and my salvation; whom shall I fear?*
*The LORD is the strength of my life; of whom shall I be afraid?*
PSALM 27:1 NKJV

## GRACE IT

Getting rid of fear is easier when you realize it's not from God. It's also easier when you understand that the Lord isn't hovering over you, scolding you for being afraid. You don't need to be hard on yourself! Grace, grace. . .accept it from Him and apply a little yourself!

Take a look at the following verse from Ephesians 1:2 (KJV): "Grace be to you, and peace, from God our Father, and from the Lord Jesus Christ." Isn't it interesting to note that grace and peace work together? Think about that. When God's grace is poured out, peace follows. And it's the kind of peace that can see you through even the most frightening times.

Also notice God chose to order the words such that *grace* comes before *peace*. This is not an accident. Before you can find peace, you must seek the grace we've already discussed. Once you've allowed grace into your life, you will find peace—not only from fear, but from all sorts of slings and arrows shot in your direction by the enemy of your soul. And trust me, dear one, the devil does *not* want to see you whole, happy, or healed. This is contrary to his purpose.

Can you do this alone? Highly unlikely, nor should you try. Fear is banished when the light of the Lord shines into the dark and scary places. Let Jesus lift His lantern and banish the fear.

*Lord, I need that kind of peace. I accept Your grace, now understanding that with it comes the ability to relax. . .to trust You through the scary times. And I don't mind admitting I've been scared, Lord. With Your help, I'm going to change my thinking. No longer will fear be my friend. I now call it what it is. . .my mortal enemy! In its place, I choose to walk in Your abundant grace. Praise You, Lord! Amen.*

## ERASE IT

Admitting your fears is a good thing. And isn't it comforting to know that even the mighty men and women from the Bible struggled with the same thing? You're definitely not alone.

Now that you've admitted you're sometimes afraid, it's time

to get really specific about the things that cause it. There's no way to erase those fears if you don't name them. The Lord will give you tools to conquer your enemies, but He wants you to take action once He does.

So what are you struggling with? Go ahead. . .admit it! As you look over the following list, ask the Lord to show you the areas where you're most vulnerable to fear. Then prepare yourself for battle!

Let's look at when you're most fearful:

- When it's time to make big decisions
- At bill-paying time
- In bed at night
- When facing obstacles or challenges
- Moving into a new home
- Dealing with job-related issues
- When faced with health problems
- Caring for the needs of your children
- When considering dating or marriage again
- Dealing with issues directly related to the divorce proceedings/dividing of assets
- Thinking about the future

Now let's look at some specific fears, so you can get more specific about what you're dealing with:

- Loss of security
- Fear of the unknown

- Fear of failure
- Financial fears
- Fear of making poor choices
- Fear of being alone
- Fear that you're not attractive to the opposite sex
- Fear that you're flawed (and different from others in some way)
- Fear of change
- Fear of things staying the same

Take a piece of paper and begin to write down both the times you're most fearful and specific things that cause you to be afraid. Don't limit yourself to things you find in this list. Instead, pray about it and ask God to reveal those triggers to you.

Are you like Ryanne, who found her fears were much worse at night than during the day?

*I had to make the conscious choice to defer my fear "until morning." Just those two words would often banish the horrible tapes that would run through my mind from the minute I laid my head on the pillow until sleep finally took over. Sometimes I would wake up during the night and be unable to go back to sleep because I'd be listing them all over again. So one night I wrote them down—all of them—then set the list aside to pray over the next day during my commute to work.*

*Sitting on the bus reading the list gave me quite a shock. Yes, I still was afraid of the future, of being alone, of financial failure, but in the morning light with the other bus riders*

*all around me I could see these were things that I could get
past with God's help. Now when I face those fears, the simple
words "until morning" go a long way toward putting them
in their place. It's not 100 percent effective yet, but I have
complete confidence someday I won't even have to say the
words. I'll just know.*

Isn't that a wonderful idea? There's something about seeing
your own words on paper that's so freeing. Once your list is
made, take the time to pray over each specific fear, then stand up
to those things with the power and the authority of Jesus Christ
inside of you. Like that cowardly lion in *The Wizard of Oz*, ask for
a dose of heavenly courage! Then, move beyond your fears to a
faith-filled life. To live, as Ryanne said, knowing the sun will rise
in the morning and God will still be there to banish the fears.

## REPLACE IT

*For God has not given us a spirit of fear,
but of power and of love and of a sound mind.*
2 TIMOTHY 1:7 NKJV

You've acknowledged your fears and even listed the ones you're
dealing with. You've started to do battle with them. Now it's
time to replace those fears with something else. Something
positive. After all, you're going to have more free time on your

hands if you're not spending it worrying and fretting.

The best replacement for fear is faith. Faith is the world's greatest mountain-mover. It kicks fear to the curb and gives you superhuman strength, spiritually and emotionally. Best of all, it's yours for the asking!

Faith is what waits in the gap between today and tomorrow. It is what covers the gaping hole left from not knowing how you'll get there. It also reminds you at every turn that the path is not one you must forge alone or without direction. Rather, faith sees what we cannot: the way to Him.

Here's a fun challenge. Open your Bible and look in the concordance. Look at the word *faith* to see how many times it's used. . .and where. Specifically, look at the places that read, "By faith so-and-so did thus-and-such." It's interesting to look at the names, isn't it? By *faith*. . .Noah built the ark. By *faith*. . . Sarah had a baby well beyond childbearing years. By *faith*. . .the Hebrew children passed through the Red Sea.

Starting to see a common theme? Some of the mightiest men and women in biblical history needed faith to get past the obstacles in their lives. Most lived in fear. . .until they garnered up the necessary faith to overcome. And even then, with faith as their guide, the fear was not banished completely. Sure, the Israelites knew the Egyptians were bearing down on them as they approached the Red Sea. Of course they were afraid. However, they kept taking steps in the right direction. If they could do it, so can you!

What you need, precious sister, is a mega-dose of faith. You need to know in your knower that God has your best interest at heart. He's going to part the seas you're facing, even if the enemy is hot on your tail. You need a reminder that things are going to get better, not worse. You have to understand that your best days are ahead. If you have that assurance, then your fears will begin to dissolve and faith will rise up in their place.

Let's take another look at that list of triggers named above. We're going to talk about how to turn your negatives into positives.

- **When it's time to make big decisions, remind yourself that even married people struggle with this one!** And think about this: There's only one answer for big decisions, and that's God's answer. So, if you're facing a huge decision, don't make it on your own. Sure, it's nice to have someone to talk with about it; but ultimately (married or not), your decision has to be God's decision. Find wise counsel, be it trusted friends or someone at church. Ask God to put people into your life who can help in this. He always does, and never too early or too late.

- **When it comes to paying bills, you need to be prepared.** Put everything down on paper. Make a plan. Having a plan will eliminate more of your fears. Even if things are tight, your carefully constructed plan will offer reassurance when fears kick in. Know what you have coming in and going out. The reality of hard numbers is much better than the fear of the concept of failing in this area. With numbers, at least you have a starting place to create a plan to improve.

- **Need to overcome nighttime fears?** Whatever you do, don't go to sleep right after working on your bills or arguing with your ex-husband on the phone. Some women find they have to stop watching the news or reading the newspaper for a season. Before you go to bed, take a warm bubble bath and spend some time listening to praise and worship music. Do you have children? If so, can you remember back to the time when you were training them to sleep at night? Learn from what you taught them by creating a routine and sticking with it. As then, don't expect the routine to work flawlessly the first night. Give it some time; prepare your heart for the night. Memorize Psalm 42:8 (KJV): "The LORD will command his lovingkindness in the day time, and in the night his song shall be with me, and my prayer unto the God of my life."

- **When facing obstacles or challenges, instead of looking at these things with dread filling your heart, get excited!** Look what you get to do! You get to speak to another mountain and watch it disappear! Before long you'll be looking forward to the unknown and not fearing it. Are you shaking your head? It's true! Just wait and see!

- **If you're facing a move to a new home, turn that move into an adventure!** Begin to praise God for your new place, even if it's not everything you hoped it would be. Resist the urge to compare it to anything you've had before. You've already learned nothing good comes from fretting over what was. It's time to focus on today. This is your place. Yours. Think about how fun it's going to be to set up your things in that new home. That excitement will override many of your fears related to the move. Perhaps you've always loved the color blue, but your husband did not. You're now free to splash it over every surface, if that's what you like. Put your stamp on your home and make it a representation of who you are becoming. Of course, there are certain obstacles to moving. A good realtor can help you make a knowledgeable choice about places to live and the going rates for them. He or she can also advise you about school districts, proximity to services, and other important issues. If you need help moving, contact your church and ask if they can assist you. Many are equipped for this very thing.

- **It's great to have a spouse to bounce your job-related woes off of, but ultimately what happens at the office gets fixed at the office.** Your job is a gift from God. Begin to praise Him for it, then watch Him take control of any challenges you might be facing there. As mentioned before, continue to pray for those who toil under the same roof as you, especially the ones who might present difficulties to you. Offer up the business and the work you do to the Lord, and watch what He does with that.

- **Caring for the needs of your children is harder when you don't have your spouse standing next to you, no**

**doubt about it.** But there's no reason to be afraid. The Lord can give you the skills if you ask Him. Seek help before a small problem becomes a big one, and watch for signs that your child is not dealing well with the divorce. Most schools have counselors who can help in this, and many will refer you to outside sources of help where you can see professionals for no or low fees. Indeed, you're now going to be called on to be both mom and dad on many days. Playing a dual role might be a challenge, but it's not an impossible one!

- **Dealing with issues directly related to the divorce proceedings or the dividing of assets?** Many fears can arise as you head into divorce court. Having an advocate is so important. A good attorney—or a friend who's already had her day in court—will bring you both comfort and courage. Know what's due you, but pray about all of it. The law is there to help you get a good start on a new life, but getting caught up in battles that serve to distract you from God's purposes is not what you should be doing at this time in your life. Choose good, godly counsel; and take steps bathed in prayer. Your feelings won't always be so close to the surface. Let others guide you and listen to their wisdom.

- **Thinking about the future?** Feeling a little scared because you don't know what's coming? Time for an attitude shift. If your best days are ahead—and they are—then the future is filled with glorious what-ifs! Yes, you read that correctly: glorious what-ifs! The Bible promises that God will never leaves us nor forsake us and that He has a plan for us. With those promises—and He is the ultimate promise keeper—how can we go wrong?

- **If you're struggling with a loss of security, remind yourself daily that your security is in the Lord.** Period. There is no other security. We can't count on a man, a job, a family, or anything else to make us secure. Even when you were married, any security you had was temporary unless it was grounded in God. The only security that matters is the "I'm sticking with God through thick and thin" kind.

- **Struggling with fear of the unknown?** Turn your hesitation into expectation! Remember. . .the unknown is known to God. And He has your best interest at heart (another of His many promises), so whatever lies around the bend is sure to be amazing!

- **Do you have an overwhelming fear of failure?** The answer is simple, really. Don't be so hard on yourself! So what if you make a mistake? So what if you fail? God will pick you back up, wipe you off, and set you on your journey once again. Some of the greatest authors of all time failed to sell their books to publishers after multiple attempts. Thank goodness they did not give up! And what about the Wright brothers? Thomas Edison? The list goes on. If you quit, you'll never know what might have happened on the very next try. Trust Him. He's big enough to handle your mishaps.

- **Financial fears?** As mentioned above, having a plan is

key. There's something about taking authority over your finances that causes you to walk victoriously over them. And don't forget to give of your time, talents, and treasures as you are able—to your local church and to others in need. This will change your perspective about money.

- **Are you terrified your future choices will be poor?**
  Maybe you're beating yourself up over this one. Perhaps you've already made quite a few poor choices along the way. Never fear! This is a new day! It's time to begin thinking about—really thinking about—those choices. Commit them to prayer. Don't make a move until you're absolutely sure you have God's take on things. His choices are the best choices. And even when you're tempted to question the outcome, you will know that you moved forward only after praying. That alone should give you the comfort you need.

- **Afraid of being alone?** When fear of abandonment kicks in, spend some quiet time with the Lord. He will remind you that He's right there. . .whether you can see Him or not.

- **Scared of change?** Remember, change isn't a bad thing. It's different, sure, but it doesn't have to be negative. If you're afraid of change, then start by changing your mind! Begin to look at the changes in your life as possibilities (get to's), not dreaded have to's.

- **Are you afraid that things might stay the same?** That nothing will ever change? Don't spend too much time fretting over this one. After all, with the other changes in your life that you didn't expect, why not believe you can expect positive ones as well? It all goes back to the Lord's promise that He has plans to prosper us and not to harm us. You might have convinced yourself that you're always going to be in the pits, but you're not! There are plenty of adventures and mountaintop experiences ahead!

Remember, daughter of God. . .fear is not your friend. It has to go. . .in Jesus' name! Don't give in to it. Rise above it!

*When the train goes through a tunnel and the*
*world gets dark, do you jump out? Of course not.*
*You sit still and trust the engineer to get you through.*
CORRIE TEN BOOM

## EMBRACE IT

Isn't it great to realize you don't have to live in fear? Even if you've spent most of your life as a fearful person, change is in the air! Embrace this new mindset. Oh, to be set free from the bondage of fear. It's like walking out of a prison cell. You'll be able to see clearly, possibly for the first time in your life. And with the Lord's help, you will walk with newfound confidence, ready to face any challenge.

The key is to lean on God—not only during this time in your life, but always. What may seem difficult at times will soon become a habit you will refer to easily. Persevere, dear one. Fear no longer has a place in your life or a hold on your heart.

As we close out this chapter, consider the following testimony from a young woman named Katie:

> *I received this verse from the Lord the day my husband deserted us. "'So do not fear, for I am with you; do not be dismayed, for I am your God. I will strengthen you and help you; I will uphold you with my righteous right hand'" Isaiah 41:10 NIV).*
>
> *I had no doubt He meant that Jesus was that "righteous right hand." I've gotten amazing comfort from that verse every time fear has crept in. I typed out that verse the day my husband left and taped it to my computer monitor.*

Doesn't that inspire you? The Lord can and will minister to you, in the very middle of your fear. And don't you love that idea. . .taping the scripture to your computer monitor? Katie was really on to something there, so follow her lead. The Bible is loaded with scriptures to help believers deal with fear, and they're yours for the asking!

Take the time to memorize the following verses. Committing these to memory is a great idea because they become weapons in your hand when you're in the middle of the battle. You can whip out one of these verses and deal with that fear head-on!

- *I sought the LORD, and he heard me, and delivered me from all my fears.*
  PSALM 34:4 KJV

- *Yea, though I walk through the valley of the shadow of death, I will fear no evil: for thou art with me; thy rod and thy staff they comfort me.*
  PSALM 23:4 KJV

- *For you did not receive a spirit that makes you a slave again to fear, but you received the Spirit of sonship. And by him we cry, "Abba, Father."*
  ROMANS 8:15 NIV

- *Do not be anxious about anything, but in everything, by prayer and petition, with thanksgiving, present your requests to God.*
  PHILIPPIANS 4:6 NIV

One more thing! Don't be disappointed in yourself if fears still pop up, even after you've done all of the things mentioned in this chapter. The enemy of your soul would love nothing more than to bring defeat, just after you've experienced victory. Don't cling to your fears. They cloud your vision. Instead, remember that every fearful moment is an opportunity to prove God's faithfulness!

*Courage is resistance to fear; mastery of fear—*
*not absence of fear.*
MARK TWAIN

# Chapter 5

## *THE DEEP STUFF*

*I would rather walk with God in the
dark than go alone in the light.*
MARY GARDINER BRAINARD

# C FACE IT

Life after divorce is filled with ups and downs, much like a roller coaster. Just about the time you go sailing over a mountaintop, you plummet down into a valley. The highs can be really high and the lows can be really low. And there's not much in between to bring a sense of steadiness. So after a divorce, you spend much of your time with that "Hang on! We're about to fly over the edge!" sensation. (Do you know that feeling?) Then, after you crest at the top of the hill, you go sailing down, down, down to the valley times. You have periods of deep anguish and pain. There, you wonder if you'll ever come back up again.

So, let's talk about those low places. If you haven't already faced at least one or two. . .you will. For the sake of this book, we're going to call them the "deep" places. The places where God wants to meet with you to do a "deep" work. Yes, those valleys are dark. Yes, they're a little scary. They can also seem never-ending.

The Lord certainly knew that we would face these deep seasons. Otherwise, why would He have dedicated an entire chapter of the Bible (the twenty-third psalm) to them? (By the way, this might be a great time to read through the twenty-third psalm once again, just to put things in perspective. It's loaded with reassuring words to prepare you for any valley experience.)

Imagine your "deep place" as a river gorge, jutting deep into the earth. It's narrow. It's dark. The river that runs through it is creepy and foreboding. As you try to maneuver its banks, your vision is limited. Down there, so far from the world above, you feel trapped and alone. You see only the shadows and hear only the echo of your own voice. At first. When the eerie call of a wolf rings out, you shiver with fear, realizing there is an evil "force" here, as well. This is an intense place, one you wish you could escape. However, the shadows surround you on every side, making it hard to see and even harder to maneuver. When you look up, up, up, you can see a hint of sunlight. But it's so far away, you wonder how you will ever bask in its glory again. No, the sunlight is only for "normal" people with "normal" lives, and you no longer meet that criterion. So, you hunker down, keep your focus on the winding riverbank, and decide to give in to the overwhelming sense that things are never going to change.

Remember that fear you just dealt with in the last chapter? Likely it struck when you were in a valley. And that loneliness you came to grips with a few chapters back? Another side effect of the valley experience. Those whispers from the enemy that you're not valuable, not worthy of love, not beautiful? All valley-speak.

And yet. . .God can use the deep seasons of your life to do a deep work, one that roots out bitterness, pain, and any unforgiveness you might still be facing. In the valley, you come face to face with yourself. There, you stand the best chance of really resolving some of your deeper, hidden issues, the things you've tucked away or avoided. And God has already promised to meet you in the valley, after all: "Even though I walk through the valley of the shadow of death, I will fear no evil, for you are with me; your rod and your staff, they comfort me" (Psalm 23:4 NIV).

When you were married, you and your husband were one flesh. When you divorced—regardless of the reason—that one flesh was ripped in two. Think about that for a moment. No wonder you go through seasons of such deep anguish. You have indeed walked through the valley of the shadow of death—the death of a marriage, the death of a dream, the death of the one-flesh experience.

Rising from the dead takes time, and lots of it. You must give yourself permission to heal. If you jump back into life pretending that everything is fine when it really isn't, it's going to catch up with you sooner or later.

Part of the healing comes after acknowledging that you struggle in the deep places, the places no one sees. And part of it comes by giving yourself permission to grieve—really grieve—the losses you've faced. . .in your way and your time. (So much for people telling you to "just get over it.")

Christian psychiatrist Paul Looney has this to say about the "deep" issues affecting women after divorce:

> Women who have struggled with depression or anxiety are even more prone to difficulty after a divorce. It is important to acknowledge and honor your feelings. The loss you experience through divorce is in many ways more difficult than losing a spouse to death. A marriage is a living thing. When it dies, grief is appropriate. Trying to push down feelings generally makes anxiety grow.
>
> Many women feel uncomfortable with feelings of anger or rage, so they try to suppress them. In the long run, this is like sitting on a submerged beach ball. You won't feel steady or comfortable for long. It is not healthy to avoid your feelings altogether; nor is it healthy to stew in them all day every day.

*I recommend spending fifteen or twenty minutes each day journaling thoughts and feelings. Getting them out on paper brings clarity and perspective. Like turning on a light in a dark room, things are less scary when you can see them clearly.*

What deep issues are you hiding away, hoping no one notices? Are you struggling with feelings of abandonment? Dealing with rejection or betrayal? Disappointment? Have you developed an "It's not fair!" attitude? If, in your heart of hearts, you're dealing with these things, it's better to acknowledge them and get them out in the open, so that the Lord can do a complete work in you. Tuck them away, and they will remain and fester.

How many times are we beaten and battered, yet rush to present ourselves to a watching world as one who "has it all together"? Often, we just want to quickly tidy up. Put our best foot forward. Put on the happy face. But devastation is often hard to hide. When you're going through a messy divorce, a struggle with anger, or a battle with depression, it's tough to pretend everything is all right.

So why do we try so hard? Why is it so difficult to let people know what we're really dealing with? Why is "vulnerability" such a difficult thing? We all go through storms, after all. We should be able to relate to one another in our moments of weakness. Perhaps it's because we feel no one else has ever hurt like we hurt. No one has ever grieved like we grieve. No one has ever felt so completely lost.

Oh, if only we could see how many times women throughout history have walked through seemingly impossible situations and come out victors in the end!

Pause for a moment to think about some of the women in the Bible who went through deep valleys. Imagine Hagar, rejected, despised, excluded. . .sent away from the father of her child and from life as she knew it. Picture how she must have felt, left alone to fend for herself. Consider the woman with the issue of blood. Her despair and desperation drove her to press through the crowd and grab the hem of Jesus' robe, no matter what others thought of her. (Desperate times call for desperate measures, right?) And what about the sinful woman, who, out of gut-wrenching emotion, knelt to soak Jesus' feet with her tears, then washed them with her hair? These women—just like you—knew what it meant to hurt. Each had to learn—in her own time and way—to acknowledge her pain and trust God to bring her through it.

Now think about Cindy, whose journey we've been following. She went through several ups and downs after her divorce. During the deeper seasons, her focus turned inward. Much of her time was spent dealing with her emotional needs. She was exhausted—from the inside out. In her weakened state, she found herself looking for comfort from a variety of sources. Food. Medication. Sleep. Television. Work. Alcohol. Relationships. You name it. She tried it.

Cindy eventually got in the groove with her work, which proved to be a nice distraction from the deep issues she'd buried. Things moved along pretty well after a while, but certain triggers would always bring up the same internal struggles. Insecurity would rise up. When she looked in the mirror, she questioned everything about her appearance. Feelings of rejection would kick in, and she wondered if any man would ever find her desirable. She inwardly struggled with anger. Though it seemed justifiable, she couldn't seem to let it go. Feelings of betrayal and frustration would consume her, long after the divorce was final and long after she thought she'd forgiven her ex-husband and others who had wronged her.

Cindy didn't invite these things. They came to the party without asking. Still, though she tried to force them away, they would not be forced. A scene from a movie. A line from a song. A glimpse of a couple through the window of a restaurant. Their "First Christmas" ornament lying in the box alongside the others that had once graced their tree. Any and all of these proved to be unexplainable triggers, sending her over the mountaintop and deep into the valley.

When it came to her children, the anguish would really set in. She continually grieved over the fact that they didn't have a strong male influence in their lives anymore. Her sons needed a father, and her daughter. . . ? How would her daughter ever find a way to pick up the pieces with her dad so far out of the picture? In the quiet times, Cindy reflected on her childhood. She remembered her parents' divorce. She remembered the pain it had caused her and wondered if her children were struggling internally as much as she had.

Things grew more complicated than ever when Cindy's ex-husband married the woman he'd been having an affair with. His new wife—the very woman who'd broken up the marriage—was now stepmom to Cindy's kids. And she seemed to slide into the role with ease. In fact, this other woman became a "buddy" to the kids; and before long, Cindy felt abandoned. . .even by her own children. She did her best to not speak ill of this woman; but when the kids spent the weekend with their father, she grieved the potential "what ifs." Of course, she would always dry her tears before the children returned home, then act as if nothing had happened.

Like many women, Cindy tucked away most of her angst and much of her pain, and forged ahead, not really dealing with things. To deal with them would be painful. And it might get ugly. So she simply pretended everything was okay when it was not. She didn't take the time to really count her losses (and it's awfully hard to grieve a loss when you don't recognize it). Because she refused to "go there," Cindy continued to struggle in her thought life. Her beliefs—about herself, about what others thought or felt—began to change.

And through it all, she just kept moving. Just kept forging ahead.

Have you ever done that? Just pasted on your prettiest smile and assured anyone who asked that you were just fine? If you say it enough, you may even convince yourself. . .in the moment. Then come the moments when you're alone, the times when family, friends, co-workers, and the church congregation are out of view. What do you tell yourself then? Is that when the tears finally fall; or, even then, do you stuff the pain back into the farthest reaches of your mind and tie it up with a big bow, never—you vow—to be opened again?

Take a look at April's story. Like many women, her pain was

so overwhelming that it caused an extreme reaction.

> *The night my second husband called from his military base in Germany to tell me he wanted a divorce to marry his pregnant girlfriend, I calmly finished the call, ate dinner with my visiting parents, put my daughter to bed, then strolled outside, sat in my car, and started to scream. The whole time I was beating every surface of the interior of the car with my fists. It was sheer rage laced with pain. Embarrassing, but true. I didn't plan to walk outside, didn't plan to get in the car. Didn't plan to go to pieces. It just happened.*
>
> *My dad heard me from inside the house and ran out to get me. I was more surprised than he was when I realized what I had done. I think this blow hit so hard because I never saw it coming.*

If you're honest with yourself, you'd have to agree. . .deep issues hurt. They hurt in the quiet times, when no one is looking. They hurt in the loud times, when you're surrounded but can't give voice to your feelings. They just plain *hurt*.

Here's the good news. We serve a deep God. He goes to the depths with us. Consider the words of Psalm 139:7–8 (NIV), which read: "Where can I go from your Spirit? Where can I flee from your presence? If I go up to the heavens, you are there; if I make my bed in the depths, you are there." You can never go to such a low place that God won't meet you there. You can never bind a pain-filled box so tightly that the Lord cannot open it and cause healing to begin. Trust Him through the deep times. . .and the deep issues.

# ⟲ GRACE IT

If you ever needed strength to truly get beyond the things that are hidden in the depths of your heart, it's now. Consider this verse from 2 Timothy 2:1 (KJV): "Thou therefore, my son, be strong in the grace that is in Christ Jesus." Think about that. Grace makes you strong. It's just what you need. . .and just in time.

How does that work exactly? Bending the knee in prayer makes you stronger, as does realizing there's nothing you can do—that it's only what He did that gives you the power to go forward. Accepting His grace is a matter of humbling yourself and admitting, "I've got to stop trying and apply what He already did."

Today, before you go one step further, take the time to ask the Lord to lavish that grace on you, that you may garner the strength to go with Him to the deep places. As you read this prayer and whisper its words, seek the Father with all your heart and with all your broken places, and know He will hear when you call.

*Lord, when I think about asking You to shine Your spotlight on the hidden places in my heart, it scares me. I don't want to go there. It's easier to just pretend everything is okay. But I know it's not. I know there are still issues to deal with. I give You permission to do that work, Father, even if it hurts. To go to the deep places. To root out the pain and replace it with Your peace. Walk me through this process, Lord. I trust You. Amen.*

# ◯ ERASE IT

*There is no pit so deep, that He is not deeper still.*
BETSIE TEN BOOM

Are you ready to take action? To dig beyond the surface? To get past the, "I'll be fine if I just don't have to think about it," stage? If so, then healing is on its way. Sure, it might take a little work, but it's work that will bring you closer to the Lord and to that exciting new life He has planned for you. Why wait? Let's get started!

Psalm 42:7 (NIV) gives us a glimpse into God's plan for healing. "Deep calls to deep in the roar of your waterfalls; all your waves and breakers have swept over me." That deep, hurting place inside you needs to call out to a deep God. Then, through the power of His Spirit, healing waves will sweep over you. . .if you let them.

It's so important to peel back the veneer and gaze into the depths of your heart, to ask the Lord to reveal the things that hurt the most. No, this won't be easy. Yes, it can change absolutely everything. You can go from living a life of pretending everything is fine to a life of healing and wholeness.

Perhaps you're not new to this process of healing. Maybe you've been covering your pain for so long the veneer won't peel. Or, worse, maybe you've forgotten where you've hidden it all. Dear one, understand that the Lord hasn't forgotten, nor will He allow you to keep what you've buried hidden, once you give Him permission to reveal it.

As you look at the list below, ask God to show you the places where healing waves need to flow. Then trust that He will do the work. . .even if it's hard.

I'm afraid that if I pull back the cobwebs covering my heart, I might see that:

- It's still beating.
- I spend a lot of time pretending things are fine when they're not.
- My recovery process is slow and disorderly.
- I'm mad at myself for not getting over this more quickly.
- I feel the need to prove myself to others.
- I feel broken and wonder if I'll ever be mended.
- I'm jealous of friends who are happily married or in good relationships.
- I secretly doubt things will ever get any better.
- I'm scared of getting healed (afraid of what that will look like).
- I've chosen to live in the valley because it's easier.
- I'm really angry that my happily-ever-after was stripped away.
- My emotions are still tied to my ex-husband.
- I enjoy being mad at "the other woman."
- I struggle to find any value or beauty in myself.
- Though I try to hide it, I still struggle with bitterness.
- I'm still finding it hard to forgive others, though I've really tried.

- I'm battling with shame and/or unconfessed sin in my life.
- I haven't forgiven myself for things I've done.
- I'm frustrated over things related to my children (i.e., custody issues and/or feelings of jealousy when they visit their father).
- I sometimes turn to things I shouldn't (food, alcohol, poor relationships) when I'm hurting.
- I overreact and/or have knee-jerk reactions (a warning sign that I still have issues to deal with).
- I'm worried about my physical health (and with good reason).
- I want to get even with those who have hurt me.
- I'm mad at God.

Even if you were only struggling with one thing from this list, healing would still take time. But it's more likely you're dealing with several issues listed above. If so, this is not the time to turn and run. Genuine healing will only come if you take one thing at a time. Acknowledge each, and trust that God—who knows you better than anyone else—will do more than slap a spiritual Band-Aid on the gaping wounds in your heart. He will, instead, offer true and lasting healing.

> *Weeping may remain for a night,*
> *but rejoicing comes in the morning.*
> PSALM 30:5 NIV

# REPLACE IT

Instead of dealing with each of the items on the list individually, we're going to handle this one differently. It's time for a crash course on going into the deep places with God. We're headed into the Holy of Holies to get real with God.

Before we do that, however, it's important to note one thing: The enemy of your soul doesn't want you to "go deep" with God. Think about that for a moment. As much as he hates the marriage of a man and woman, he hates the marriage of Christ and the church even more. So he works overtime to pull you—the bride of Christ—away from your groom. He always wants to keep you from entering the Holy of Holies because he knows what will happen once you enter. But never fear! As soon as you enter that secret, holy place with your heavenly Father, the enemy slithers away in the grass, knowing he's met his match.

If you've never done a study of the Holy of Holies, this would be a great time to do so. In Old Testament times, the people of God had to rely on animal sacrifice as an atonement for their sin. Once a year, the high priest would go into a tiny room called the Holy of Holies (or "Most Holy Place") to represent the people and to lay their sins on the altar before God. This small room was an inner sanctuary of the tabernacle. Only the man of God was welcome inside.

The Holy of Holies was a set-apart place and, in many respects, a fearful place—for the priest symbolically carried in the sins, anguishes, and pains of the people.

Think about that high priest for a moment. Can you hear

his heart thumping as he pushes back the veil and enters that inner sanctum? Can you see his hands shaking as he burns the incense and sprinkles sacrificial animal blood? Can you sense the relief as the ritual comes to its completion? Must've been pretty heavy stuff—to come in with so many sins on your hands.

If you're a blood-bought believer of Jesus Christ, you recognize that His work on the cross was the final payment for our sins. He paid it all on Calvary. And (what an awesome story this is!) just after He died, the veil in the temple was torn in two. No longer do you have to be a high priest to enter the Most Holy Place. God desires that all of us—scarred, exhausted, sinful, tainted people—enter. Why? Not to atone for our sins. No, Jesus took care of that part for us. We are now invited into the Holy of Holies for personal, intimate time with the Lord of the universe. The only sacrifice He wants from us is a sacrifice of praise. . .a bending of our knee and our will.

Picture yourself walking into the throne room of God, His Most Holy Place. Imagine coming with your heart in your hands and laying it on the altar so that He can do His perfect work. Consider the condition of that heart as you openly expose your deepest wounds, your most painful experiences. Then, watch in awe as your Savior takes your heart in His gentle hands, reshapes and remolds it, then breathes new life over your situation, offering healing, hope, and grace.

We don't have to be afraid of God. That's it in a nutshell. There's no reason to fear getting real with Him. You can bare your soul, and you won't be rejected. You can share your angst, your pain, your deepest longings; and He will sweep you into His arms. He already sees the anger or frustration you're carrying. There's nothing you can say or do that will shock Him. In fact, He already knows. He's just waiting for you to come into that Holy Place so that true healing can begin.

What are you bringing to Him today? Let's offer up the things on our list as sacrifices to the Lord.

- Lord, I'm afraid that if I pull back the cobwebs covering my heart, I might see that it's still beating. Oh, but Father, I thank You for a beating heart. I thank You that my life goes on, and that it's a better life than ever before! I trust You to do a complete work in me.
- Father, I've spent a lot of time pretending things are fine when they're not. I give that urge to You. No more pretending, Lord. Those days are behind me. I'm getting real, no matter how difficult that might be.
- Lord, I know that my recovery process has been slow and disorderly at times. Thank You for reminding me that that's okay. Progress is progress. I'm grateful for each step, even the messy ones.
- Father, I've been really mad at myself for not getting over this more quickly. I want to just snap my fingers and be done with this. Oh, but Lord, I know You want to do a deep work in me. Thank You for guiding me through it, even when it's painful.
- I feel the need to prove myself to others sometimes, Lord. I don't know why. Maybe it's because I feel like I've failed in my marriage and need to prove that I have value, that

something I do will work out. Help me see that I don't have to "earn" Your love or the love of others. I'm so grateful that You love me, even when I'm incapable of doing anything at all.

- Father, there are so many times when I feel broken. In fact, I wonder if I'll ever be mended. In those times, remind me of the work You've already done. May I see the healing, every step of the way. And may hope rise up within me!

- This is a hard one to admit, Lord, but I'm jealous of friends who are happily married or in good relationships. When I'm with them, please calm my troubled spirit. Help me to see them for what they are. . .examples of godly relationships.

- Father, in the quiet times, I secretly doubt things will ever get any better. I've done a pretty good job of hiding this hopeless feeling from others. But You and I know better. Oh, Lord, I need Your perspective on this! I need to know in my "knower" that this valley won't last forever. Give me glimpses of sunlight, Lord. Take away any fear about my healing. And get me beyond the mindset that living in the valley is somehow easier.

- Lord, I confess my anger to you. I'm really mad that my happily-ever-after was stripped away. I know that this is righteous anger, but pray it won't lead to sin. Take away any bitterness, Father. I give it all to You today. Keep me from giving in to knee-jerk reactions. Guard my heart when it comes to thoughts and attitudes about my ex-husband and/or his new girlfriend/wife. I want my heart to be honorable, Lord.

- Father, this is a hard one to confess. . .and maybe I feel this way because of what I've been through, but I sometimes struggle to find any value or beauty in myself. Help me to see myself as You see me: a lovely child of the King!

- I'm frustrated over things related to my children (i.e., custody issues and/or feelings of jealousy when they visit their father). Lord, if I ever needed Your perspective, it's now. I don't want to have knee-jerk reactions or act out of bitterness. Help me through this particular valley, Lord. May I represent You so that my children see me as a godly example.

- Father, this is a hard one to confess, too, but I sometimes turn to things I shouldn't (food, alcohol, poor relationships) when I'm hurting. I need Your help to get beyond this. I can't do this on my own. Give me ideas for things I can do to redirect my thinking when temptations come. I give this area of my life to You, Lord. Please help me.

- Father, please guard my physical health. Sometimes I worry that this experience will be the death of me. I fear major health complications as a result of my worries and fears. Release me—both from the worries and fears, and from any health-related problems. Help me to garner the strength to take care of myself, even when I don't feel like it.

- Lord, this is the toughest of all. I've openly forgiven my ex-husband for a variety of things before; but today, I lay him—and our former relationship—on the altar. I openly confess my unforgiveness today. Help me in this area, Lord. May I set him (and/or his girlfriend/wife) free, so that I may be set free.

Dear child of God, once you've gone through this list, take any other concerns and thoughts to the Lord. Don't just scratch the surface. Go deep with Him, especially if you're battling with shame or unconfessed sin. Get those things out in the open.

Any time you begin to deal with deep issues, take a step into the Holy of Holies. God is already there, waiting. . .with healing in His wings. Get real with your Daddy, God, about the things that hurt you. He's there to bring healing when you do.

*God brings men into deep waters,*
*not to drown them, but to cleanse them.*
JOHN AUGHEY

## ◯ EMBRACE IT

Only God can satisfy the longing of your soul. But He has to draw you away to a secret, quiet place to do so. Consider the story of Ann, who shares from the depth of her experience:

> *I married young, filled with hope for the future. Within four years, I'd given birth to three children. My husband and I were both believers, but he always seemed to have a wandering eye. I came into the marriage with unresolved issues toward my father, who had left my mother for another woman. This exaggerated the trust issues between my husband and me.*
>
> *Before long, he began to leave for weeks or months at a time to be with other women. I always took him back, too insecure and scared to think I could survive without him. My worst fears came true when my husband was served with a paternity suit. He had fathered not one, but two children with one of the women he'd been involved with. This news literally sent me into shock.*
>
> *In spite of this, I still remained in the marriage, convinced God would turn things around. Unfortunately, my husband's unfaithfulness continued. I finally garnered the courage to leave. I knew I had biblical grounds, and my pastor and church family supported me. The healing began with their encouragement.*
>
> *Years have passed, and I'm finally dealing with the hurts and wounds of the past. It takes a long time to mend from such deep and personal wounds, after all. But I've finally*

*"gotten real" with God and allowed Him to dig into the cobweb-filled corners of my life. Now I feel like I have a second lease on life. He has truly turned my mourning into dancing, and I will never be able to thank Him enough.*

Do you see, dear one? Even the deepest, darkest pain can be turned around. God can and will use it for His glory. Allow Him to go to the deep places. What you will receive, in response, is a deep, abiding joy. So, step into the Holy of Holies today. Enter into that secret place.

There are a host of scriptures to support this personal, one-on-one encounter with the Lord. If you're struggling—wondering if it's safe to really bare your soul, to get real about the things that still cause pain—take a look at the following scriptures.

- *Then Jesus uttered another loud cry and breathed his last. And the curtain in the sanctuary of the Temple was torn in two, from top to bottom.*
  MARK 15:37–38 NLT

- *When Christ came as high priest of the good things that are already here, he went through the greater and more perfect tabernacle that is not man-made, that is to say, not a part of this creation. He did not enter by means of the blood of goats and calves; but he entered the Most Holy Place once for all by his own blood, having obtained eternal redemption.*
  HEBREWS 9:11–12 NIV

- *Therefore, since we have been justified through faith,
  we have peace with God through our Lord Jesus Christ,
  through whom we have gained access by faith into this
  grace in which we now stand.*
  ROMANS 5:1–2 NIV

- *Therefore, brothers, since we have confidence to enter the Most
  Holy Place by the blood of Jesus, by a new and living way opened
  for us through the curtain, that is, his body, and since we have
  a great priest over the house of God, let us draw near to God
  with a sincere heart in full assurance of faith, having our hearts
  sprinkled to cleanse us from a guilty conscience and having our
  bodies washed with pure water. Let us hold unswervingly to the
  hope we profess, for he who promised is faithful.*
  HEBREWS 10:19–23 NIV

- *He who dwells in the shelter of the Most High will rest in
  the shadow of the Almighty. I will say of the LORD, "He is
  my refuge and my fortress, my God, in whom I trust."*
  PSALM 91:1–2 NIV

- *My dove, that art in the clefts of the rock, in the secret places
  of the stairs, let me see thy countenance, let me hear thy voice;
  for sweet is thy voice, and thy countenance is comely.*
  SONG OF SOLOMON 2:14 KJV

Jesus stands ready, waiting for you to come. Allow yourself
to be completely vulnerable, even if it's the hardest thing you've
ever done. Peel back the veneer and expose the very things you've

hidden away. You can trust the Lord with your pain, no matter how intense. Go to Him. . .with your burdens, your hurts, your deepest fears. He paid a heavy price so that you could come into that secret place. Today, He asks only one thing: Come.

*It is not the mountain we conquer but ourselves.*
EDMUND HILLARY

# Chapter 6

# *It's All about Choices*

*God asks no man whether he will accept life. That is not the choice.*
*You must take it. The only choice is how.*
HENRY WARD BEECHER

# ⊂ FACE IT

There are some things in life we don't get to choose. Likely, you didn't choose for your marriage to crumble. Maybe you didn't choose to be single. You might not have chosen for your finances to end up in a whirlwind state or your emotions to be shaken. No, we don't always get to choose. That's why—when we do— it's so important to make the right choices.

Remember that "Eeny, meeny, miny, moe" game you used to play? Chances are pretty good you're still playing it, if you're separated or divorced. You're probably facing more choices now than ever, and making the right ones isn't as easy as some might think. For example, "How do I perceive myself, now that I'm divorced?" is a tricky one. And, "Do I have it inside me to forgive those I need to forgive?" is another. Once you get past those, there are the everyday choices, like, "Which do I pay this week—the electric bill or my car payment?" or "What do I do with my hour of free time today—mow the lawn or read a book?" Whether you're dealing with something internal and personal or something mundane and commonplace, the choice won't always be clear.

Or maybe you're dealing with so many choices that you merely shut down and decide to choose none of them. That, dear one, is a choice, too.

Still, with God guiding you—and He is—you have a good running start.

Think of all the choices you've made over the past weeks and months. You've chosen to trust the Lord, to believe Him to see you through this. You've chosen to be nice and play fair. (That hasn't always been easy, has it?) You've chosen not to react in a knee-jerk fashion (or maybe you've chosen to forgive yourself when you messed up). You've chosen to protect yourself—physically, emotionally, and psychologically. You've made the choice not to use your children as pawns. You've made up your mind to see men as individuals, not lump them all into one group. You've made the decision not to be bitter. And, most importantly, you've chosen to look forward, not back.

But if you've been the queen of poor choices up to this point, don't fret. You're not alone. Some of the greatest people in the Bible made really poor choices. Remember Sarah? She enlisted her maid, Hagar, to sleep with her husband, Abraham, so that he would have an offspring. Think of Tamar, who chose to prostitute herself and ended up having a child by her father-in-law. Consider Lot's wife. . .who made the monumental mistake of looking back instead of forward.

No, you are definitely not alone when it comes to any poor choices you might have made. And even if you've made some really bad ones in the past, the future is stretched out before you, a welcome mat for change.

So it's time to make great choices. Of course, one of the first ones you'll have to make is the choice to cut the emotional ties to your ex-husband. Take a look at what Shelley Stile, Divorce Recovery Life Coach, says in her article "Dealing with Your Ex After Divorce and Setting Boundaries":

*Your divorce decree is only step one in moving into a*

*new life after divorce. The real divorce is the cutting off
of the emotional, mental, and physical ties that still bind
you to your ex-husband. This is the real work of divorce
recovery: becoming a single woman possessed of confidence,
self-esteem, an enthusiasm for life, and, most important, a
complete break from the emotional turmoil that led to your
divorce in the first place.*

*All too often, women experience the same conflicts with
their ex that originally led to divorce: constant arguments,
reactive behavior leading to emotional upsets, old patterns
of reliance, the barrage of destructive barbs aimed at your
self-esteem, and deep hurts. To truly be divorced you must
put forth great effort and inner work that will sever your
ties to your ex, and you must build a structure that will
facilitate that work. [2]*

Great advice. Breaking that "soul tie" to the man you
planned to spend a lifetime with is hard work. Maybe you're
accustomed to depending on him to help you make other
choices (housing, car, job-related). He used to be the first
person you would call. It's time to find another first responder!
(Thankfully, the Lord makes a terrific first responder. And a
good friend will make a great second responder.) Once you
break that tie to your ex, you're freed up to make some of the
best choices of your life!

So, how do you shift from making poor choices to good

---

[2] Shelley Stile, "Dealing With Your Ex After Divorce and Setting Boundaries"
www.womansdivorce.com/ex-after-divorce.html

ones? Let's look at Cindy to see how she managed.

When Cindy and her husband separated, she chose to believe that God would reconcile her to her husband. She prayed in that direction. In fact, she remained soul-tied to him for quite a long time. Unfortunately, her husband chose to go a different direction and ended up divorcing her and quickly marrying someone else. Cindy tried to hang on to her feelings for him (and her emotional ties to him), but didn't confess that to anyone but herself.

At this point, Cindy's pain caused her to make some really poor choices. First, she chose to hide herself away from people who genuinely cared for her. Next, she chose to hold onto the bitterness and pain her husband's actions had caused. During this season, a spiritual wall went up between Cindy and the Lord. She blamed Him for not stopping the pain and chose—as a result—to pull away from church and the Word.

Cindy's bitterness served as a catalyst for her next choice: to not take care of herself. Before long, she was eating the wrong foods and not sleeping properly. In this newly exhausted state, she chose to look at herself as a failure. Her marriage had failed, after all. Pretty soon, she could hardly keep up with her work. She began to wonder if she would fail in that area, too. Now seeing herself in a defeated state, she chose to withdraw from healthy relationships.

With the haze of emotions leading the way, Cindy eventually made the poorest choice of all. When temptation presented itself, she jumped in headfirst. Cindy chose to enter a rebound relationship with a man she barely knew, hoping she would find the answers she sought in his arms. After all, he whispered sweet nothings in her ear and told her she had value.

It didn't take long for Cindy to realize she'd made a mistake. She ended up breaking off the relationship. This was one of the best choices she'd made in a while. Slowly, but surely, she began to choose a better future for herself, starting by recommitting her life to the Lord. That sparked a new desire to care for herself—physically and emotionally. Caring for herself gave Cindy the strength she needed to make better choices with her finances and her emotions. In this refreshed state, she was finally able to enter into healthy relationships and to keep up with her busy workload.

Have you walked a mile in Cindy's shoes? Do you know what it is to choose bitterness as a lifestyle? Have you allowed walls to rise up between yourself and the Lord? Have you chosen poor relationships—either toxic friendships or rebound relationships with men? If so, it's not too late to make the best choice of all. . . to return to the Lord and to trust Him with your future.

This is not the time to look back and ponder all of the things you've done wrong. On the contrary, this is the time to implement a plan of action, with your choices clearly defined. The Lord stands before you today, offering the decision of all decisions: "Choose for yourselves this day whom you will serve" (Joshua 24:15 NIV).

Before you ponder all of the many choices, choose a relationship with the One who knows you best and loves you most.

*Forget past mistakes. Forget failures.*
*Forget everything except what you're going to do now and do it.*
WILLIAM DURANT

# GRACE IT

If there was ever a time to understand God's grace, it's after you've made a few poorly thought-out choices. (That is not to imply that your choices led to your divorce; simply that you've probably made a few blunders along the way.) Instead of looking back and beating yourself up, why not accept that grace and move forward? Consider the words found in James 4:6 (NIV): "But he gives us more grace. That is why Scripture says: 'God opposes the proud but gives grace to the humble.'" Anytime you choose to humble yourself—a terrific choice, by the way—God extends more grace. Why not spend some time with Him right now, humbling yourself and dealing with some of your choices, good and bad?

*Lord, I've made some mistakes in the past. Some of my choices weren't great. I humbly come to You, asking for grace to make better decisions in the future. I want the years that are ahead of me to be better than the years that are behind me. I need your grace to make that happen. Help me make the best possible choices—today and always. Amen.*

# ⟲ ERASE IT

*Pain is inevitable. Suffering is optional.*
M. KATHLEEN CASEY

So, you've made a few poor choices. Admitting it, as we've already seen, is a good thing. Past decisions—even bad ones—propel you to make better ones in the future. Take a close look at some of the tougher choices facing women who've been through a divorce. Which ones do you struggle with?

- Choosing to see yourself as a success instead of a failure
- Choosing to believe God is good
- Choosing to believe God has your best interest at heart
- Choosing to believe you are beautiful to the Lord and to others
- Choosing to believe you have a hope and a future
- Choosing to relinquish pain and bitterness
- Choosing to forgive
- Choosing to do the right thing as it relates to child custody issues
- Choosing to live at peace as a single person
- Choosing your identity in Christ and not in a man
- Choosing to reset your expectations
- Choosing to maintain healthy relationships
- Choosing to avoid toxic friendships
- Choosing to avoid inappropriate relationships with the opposite sex

- Choosing to eat the right foods
- Choosing not to lash out at your ex-husband
- Choosing not to lump all men into one category
- Choosing to believe you still have value
- Choosing to resist the enemy
- Choosing not to drag your kids into your pain
- Choosing to make good financial decisions
- Choosing not to panic
- Choosing not to wallow in self-pity
- Choosing not to let your anger lead to sin
- Choosing to balance work and rest
- Choosing to dream again
- Choosing victory instead of defeat
- Choosing to embrace the "new normal"

When it comes to choices, there are six little letters that can change your life forever: D-E-C-I-D-E. Decide. Make up your mind. No turning back. A choice is simply that: a choice. It requires something more than hoping. . .it requires a decision. And the only way to truly decide something is to have the mind of Christ. To see things the way He sees them.

Are you ready, daughter of God? Ready to make some choices that will change your life forever? If so, pause and spend some time asking for the Lord's direction before you read another word. Focus on 1 Corinthians 2:16 (NIV): "'For who has known the mind of the Lord that he may instruct him?' But we have the mind of Christ."

After you've spent some time in prayer, be prepared for some life-changing choices!

# C REPLACE IT

*What lies behind us and what lies before us are tiny matters
compared to what lies within us.*
RALPH WALDO EMERSON

There's something about getting God's perspective on our
choices that gives us strength to make better ones. And there's
no better time than the present to do so. It is no accident that
you are reading this book—right here, right now. The Lord, out
of His great love for you—wants to give you an opportunity to
let go of the past and turn toward the rest of your life. But that
requires action from you. Action and determination.

What does action look like for you? Maybe it comes through
praying about what to do. Or maybe you already know what
the Lord is asking, and the action is in carrying out that plan. In
whatever case you find yourself, determination will be the key to
seeing the action through. Don't let the enemy of your soul talk
you out of taking action!

Read over this list, silently at first. Then, after you've gone
through it, pick out the ones that apply to your life and speak
them aloud. They are written in first person so that you can
both hear and apply the words to your life. The items on this list
represent God's mind for you, His child.

- **I choose to believe that I am not a failure and that I
  have value.** I will stand on the words of Proverbs 16:3
  (NIV), which reads: "Commit to the LORD whatever you
  do, and your plans will succeed."

- **I choose to believe that God is good.** I refuse to buy into the lie that the enemy whispered in Eve's ear in the Garden of Eden, when he implied that God was somehow stingy or selfish. I don't ever want to doubt God's goodness. Instead, I choose to believe the words of Psalm 107:31 (KJV), which reads: "Oh that men would praise the LORD for his goodness, and for his wonderful works to the children of men!"

- **I choose to believe that God has my best interest at heart.** He knew me before the foundation of the world and loves me. God's plans for me are beyond what I could ask for or think. "Even before he made the world, God loved us and chose us in Christ to be holy and without fault in his eyes" (Ephesians 1:4 NLT).

- **Though it might be hard, I choose to relinquish the pain and bitterness I feel toward my ex-husband or anyone else I've been holding in bondage.** I will be "better" and not "bitter." And while I'm forgiving others, I also choose to forgive myself for any role I might have played in the breakup of my marriage. I trust in the words found in Mark 11:25 (NIV): " 'And when you stand praying, if you hold anything against anyone, forgive him, so that your Father in heaven may forgive you your sins.' "

- **I make a conscious choice to live at peace as a single person.** My identity is found in Christ and not in a man. I choose contentment in my current state. I trust that the words in Isaiah 26:3 (NIV) are true: "You will keep in perfect peace him whose mind is steadfast, because he trusts in you."

- **I choose to reset my expectations, letting go of any sadness or feelings of loss, as I am able.** I trust God with my expectations. "What is more, I consider everything a loss compared to the surpassing greatness of knowing Christ Jesus my Lord, for whose sake I have lost all things. I consider them rubbish, that I may gain Christ and be found in him" (Philippians 3:8–9 NIV).

- **I make up my mind to choose healthy relationships.** I will avoid inappropriate relationships with the opposite sex and will draw near to those who draw me closer to the Lord, recognizing the important role they will play in my life during this season. "Perfume and incense bring joy to the heart, and the pleasantness of one's friend springs from his earnest counsel" (Proverbs 27:9 NIV).

- **I choose to live at peace with all men.** This might mean I have to occasionally make concessions. I refuse to get caught up in a tug-of-war where my child is caught in the middle. I will pick my battles carefully and do all I can to let my love shine through—to all involved. "And let the peace of God rule in your hearts, to which also you were called in one body; and be thankful" (Colossians 3:15 NKJV).

- **I choose to step away from toxic friendships. . .those friendships that lead me away from the Lord and cause me to stumble.** "Don't you know that friendship with the world is hatred toward God? Anyone who chooses to be a friend of the world becomes an enemy of God" (James 4:4 NIV).

- **I will do my best to choose a church home if I don't already have one, and will seek the godly counsel or teaching I need to get through this season.** I will keep in mind the words from Hebrews 10:24–25 (NASB), which reads: "And let us consider how to stimulate one another to love and good deeds, not forsaking our own assembling together, as is the habit of some, but encouraging one another; and all the more as you see the day drawing near."

- **I choose not to drag my children into my pain.** I will lead by example, so that my kids can one day make good choices themselves. I want them to see that my choices were made out of love, not out of pain, anger, or fear. "Like a city whose walls are broken down is a man who lacks self-control" (Proverbs 25:28 NIV).

- **I choose to care for my physical body.** It is the temple of the Lord, and I want to keep it in the best possible shape. I also choose to balance work and rest to the best of my ability. "Do you not know that your body is a temple of the Holy Spirit who is in you, whom you have from God, and that you are not your own? For you have been bought with a price: therefore glorify God in your body" (1 Corinthians 6:19–20 NASB).

- **I choose to stop focusing on my physical appearance— good, bad, or otherwise.** Whether others find me to be a great beauty or not, I am God's beloved daughter and exquisite in His sight. True beauty is inward, not outward. Outward beauty fades away, but inner beauty does not. I choose to spend this season of my life becoming a beauty queen—from the inside out. "Charm is deceitful and beauty is passing, but a woman who fears the LORD, she shall be praised" (Proverbs 31:30 NKJV).

- **I choose to not lash out at my ex-husband or others, even when provoked.** I will do my best to think before speaking and to "act" instead of "reacting." "Let the words of my mouth, and the meditation of my heart, be acceptable in thy sight, O LORD, my strength, and my redeemer" (Psalm 19:14 KJV).

- **I choose to see men as individuals and not lump them all into one category.** The heart and actions of one man cannot be compared to the heart and actions of another. "A wise man's heart is at his right hand; but a fool's heart at his left" (Ecclesiastes 10:2 KJV).

- **I choose to resist the enemy.** I understand that his ultimate desire is to steal, kill, and destroy. He would love nothing better than to separate me from my God and convince me I have no value. I refuse those lies, in Jesus' name. And I choose not to willfully enter into sin, no matter how tempting. "But if you do not do what is right, sin is crouching at your door; it desires to have you, but you must master it" (Genesis 4:7 NIV).

- **I choose to trust God with my finances and to ask for His help making good financial decisions.** I will remember the words of Psalm 37:25 (NIV), which read:

"I was young and now I am old, yet I have never seen the righteous forsaken or their children begging bread."

- **I choose not to panic, even when I'm on the frontlines of the battle.** Instead, I will stand strong. "Finally, my brethren, be strong in the Lord, and in the power of his might. Put on the whole armour of God, that ye may be able to stand against the wiles of the devil" (Ephesians 6:10–11 KJV).

- **I choose not to let my anger and frustration lead to sin.** I will not let the sun go down on my anger. "Be ye angry, and sin not: let not the sun go down upon your wrath" (Ephesians 4:26 KJV).

- **I choose not to wallow in self-pity.** Oh, it's tempting, for sure. But instead of moaning and groaning over all of the ways my spouse failed to live up to my expectations (and/or my idea of what God's expectations were), I choose to leave that in God's hands and deal with what I can do something about: myself and my attitudes. " 'I will leave off my sad countenance and be cheerful' " (Job 9:27 NASB).

- **I choose to dream again—wonderful, glorious dreams of a bright, hopeful future.** I choose to blossom as a flower, living as who I was meant to be in Christ, becoming all He wants me to be. In short, I choose to thrive and not just survive! God can do more than I ask or think! "Now to him who is able to do immeasurably more than all we ask or imagine, according to his power that is at work within us, to him be glory in the church and in

Christ Jesus throughout all generations, for ever and ever! Amen" (Ephesians 3:20–21 NIV).

- **More important than any other choice I will ever make, I choose Christ.** I acknowledge His position as Lord and Savior of my life and His amazing work on the cross. I understand that this is the most important choice of my life. I believe the words of Romans 3:22–25 (NIV), which read: "This righteousness from God comes through faith in Jesus Christ to all who believe. There is no difference, for all have sinned and fall short of the glory of God, and are justified freely by his grace through the redemption that came by Christ Jesus. God presented him as a sacrifice of atonement, through faith in his blood."

Congratulations, woman of God! Today, you have made life-changing choices. Over the next month or so, read this list daily. Out loud. With authority. You will be surprised at how much easier it will be to make good decisions when you're speaking with such boldness.

## C EMBRACE IT

Every day, you stand at a fork in the road and face decisions. What a privilege, to know the Creator of the universe stands alongside you, helping you make the right choices. When His thoughts are your thoughts, you can truly step out with confidence.

As we end this chapter on choices, take a look at a woman who had to go through major changes, both in her attitude and in several other areas of her life.

Consider Tammi's story:

> *My husband wasn't ideal, but whose is? When he left, I struggled with finding who I was without him. We never went anywhere or did anything, in or out of the church, because he refused. In the blink of an eye, I'd gone from making excuses for him to having no excuse.*
>
> *Now I had to choose to be who the Lord meant me to be. That was scary, but the thing that really propelled me forward was a question a wise friend asked one day out of the blue: "Tammi, do you realize if God's given you something to do and you ignore Him, you're walking in disobedience? Worse, He will find someone else to get it done; and you'll miss out on the blessings."*
>
> *Well, that really got my attention. It's been almost six months since she asked me that question. I'm a regular volunteer in the church preschool program on Sunday mornings, and just last week I joined a bowling league. A bowling league! Me!*

Regardless of where you've come from, you can make great choices in the days and months ahead. The following scriptures will help you in your journey:

- *Let this mind be in you, which was also in Christ Jesus.*
  PHILIPPIANS 2:5 KJV

- *And if it seem evil unto you to serve the LORD, choose you this day whom ye will serve; whether the gods which your fathers served that were on the other side of the flood, or the gods of the Amorites, in whose land ye dwell: but as for me and my house, we will serve the LORD.*
  JOSHUA 24:15 KJV

- *And be not conformed to this world: but be ye transformed by the renewing of your mind, that ye may prove what is that good, and acceptable, and perfect, will of God.*
  ROMANS 12:2 KJV

Sometimes we are too timid or scared to choose "the best." We fear we can't achieve it. I think we have to believe that God only wishes us the best; and if we leave the outcome to Him, we will deliver the best because it will be God's choice.

In this life, we're given the freedom to choose (in good times and in bad). God doesn't want us to shuffle our responsibility off onto others. In other words, you're the only one who can make the right choices for you. That's not to say you shouldn't seek counsel; but ultimately, you have to go with what you think the

Lord is telling you to do.

With Him leading the way, it is possible to make good choices, even if you're walking through a difficult season. As long as we are listening for His guidance and make choices based on what He tells us to do, we can build a bridge to our future made of faith that God will keep the road under our feet and guide us on the path we should take. Ultimately, He will deliver the best because it will be *God's* choice.

As we close out this section, consider the words of Helen Keller, who certainly knew her share of trials and tribulations. Take a look at how she made her choices. What a great life motto:

> *To think clearly without hurry or confusion;*
> *To love everybody sincerely;*
> *To act in everything with the highest motives;*
> *To trust God unhesitatingly.*
> HELEN KELLER

# Chapter 7

## *Calgon, Take Me Away!*

*Blessed is the person who is too busy to worry in the daytime*
*and too sleepy to worry at night.*
UNKNOWN

## C FACE IT

Keep on keepin' on!

One of the toughest things about being single again is that those pesky day-to-day things move forward and must be handled, whether you want to or not. Everyday tasks, once simple, are often problematic for women in transition. Paying bills. Cooking dinner. Eating dinner. Feeding the dog. Cleaning toilets. Going to work every day. Sleeping. Bathing. Dressing. Breathing.

You get the idea. Nothing stops the world from turning or the grass from growing. Work doesn't go away just because you wish it did.

In fact, the mundane things of life go on, despite any physical or emotional challenges you might be facing. It's like someone forgot to tell the electric company you're going through a major shift in your life. They just keep sending the bill, regardless of how you're feeling. And the backed-up toilet? It doesn't care that you're traumatized. It just needs fixing. The wheels of life keep turning, whether you're ready for the ride or not.

If you're having a hard time jumping back into life, you're in good company. Several of the great men and women from the Bible faced the temptation to curl up under the covers. Remember David. . .hiding in the cave? And what about Jonah. . .doing anything and everything he could to avoid doing the one thing he should? Think about Elijah. Didn't he plop down under a Broom Tree and hope to die in that very spot?

These poor souls faced exactly what you're facing now. . .the inability to function normally in a fast-paced world after facing a traumatic situation. It was easier for them to just stop. Forget about life. Zone out. Give up.

Oh, but that's impossible! Life is for the living! And the everyday things are a gift, not a curse. Seeing them as such will change everything! Why go through the emotional healing we've talked about in prior chapters, if not to jump back into life again?

So, you need to get back to business. . .but it's a challenge. You'd rather just take some time to yourself. Forget about things. Watch TV. Eat Oreos. Wear the same nightgown that hasn't been washed in days. Instead, you're faced with laundry, dirty dishes, work-related e-mails, and the never-ending stack of bills. And if you have kids at home, you're inundated with things related to their daily lives, too. Ball games. Trips to the grocery store. Carpool. You name it! Life goes on, even when you wish you could just hide under a rock.

If there was ever a time to cry out, "Calgon, take me away!" it's now. Unfortunately, a bubble bath is about all you're going to get at this stage of the game. . .and not a very long one. There's no time to sneak away. You can't retreat. It's time to roll up those sleeves and get back into the game of life.

So draw the bath, sink into the bubbles, and read a good book; or, even better, spend some time in prayer. Seek respite for a few moments, but know the real work is still ahead and in need of doing.

Poor Cindy. She had a hard time with this one. Because she was self-employed, no one nudged her to get the work done. So, she started slipping. One thing led to another, and before long, she was behind on several projects. For a while, she didn't care. After all, she was still struggling with some of the fears and abandonment issues we've already discussed. Why did it matter if she got the work done? Who was paying attention, anyway? She developed the same attitude about paying bills. Did it really matter that the car payment was a couple of weeks late? Let them come and get it. She didn't really care, anyway.

Does this sound familiar? It's easy to slip into the mindset of thinking you're the Lone Ranger with no one watching and no one to be accountable to. This is an illusion, of course, as there are always consequences and always responsibilities. Cindy knew this, and yet it was just so easy to ignore the facts that were right in front of her. Unfortunately, the depression kept her frozen, unable to get things done.

As you can imagine, Cindy drifted along in this mindset for a while, but eventually reached a point where reality hit. To her surprise, it looked like people were paying attention, after all. "Get to work or lose everything you've worked for," was pretty much her life's theme song. A strong statement, to be sure, but sometimes that's what we need, isn't it? Sometimes a firm nudge just won't do it.

Cindy faced her fears and made the journey into the Holy of Holies. There, she found not only the necessary emotional and spiritual healing she longed for, but also the strength necessary to face life again. In fact, she found more than that. She found the *desire* to return to life once again.

So, back to work Cindy went. It was tough at first, but she eventually got back in the groove. In fact, she found that the work provided just the right opportunity to stay busy and stop fretting over the negatives in her life.

There's something about being busy that does this. Idle hands are the devil's tools. Thus goes the old saying. Cindy could tell you how very true that sentiment is. The Lord used her job to help settle her mind and heart. Before long, she realized the routine of working was the best prescription for what ailed her. And that workload at home—the laundry and so forth? It, too, helped ease the pain, in its own mysterious way. Having something ordinary to do felt familiar, comforting.

It also filled her time with productive things. Remember that list you used to help navigate your way through the fog? Now you can use it to check off the things you've done. (Thank God for healing! You're freed up to actually get back in the game of life!) The feeling of accomplishment is just one benefit. The fact that things are actually getting done will begin to clear the confusion in your world and also move you forward toward a more organized life. And at this point, organization—if you can manage it—is key.

So, what about you? Are you still coasting along, but not really accomplishing anything? Having a hard time getting your groove back? Wishing you could retreat to a Caribbean beach for some fun-in-the-sun time instead of driving back and forth to the office? Or has diving back into your work given you the escape you need from any negatives in your life?

Face it. . .it's hard to think about work when your mind is cluttered with thoughts related to a breakup. It's especially hard if you've moved to a new home and can't even find your clothes and shoes because you haven't had time or energy to unpack. But getting back to work is critical to your survival—not just financially, but psychologically, as well.

Don't depend on your feelings to find the proper time to do these things. At this point in your recovery, your feelings are going to change as quickly as the other things in your life. Rather, know you must do something—anything—besides sitting still and waiting for the feeling to strike.

Maybe you can relate to Lisa's story:

> *It seemed I was on autopilot for months. I went through the motions of life to survive. I woke up, went to work, and came home. Then I would watch brain-numbing TV and sleep on the couch. I guess it was actually like I was surviving a trauma or family illness. I just went through the motions and tried not to really think. It was easier that way.*
>
> *I'm also the type of person where everything is fine. . . on the outside. No one would have ever known I was going through a divorce. In fact, everyone at my former job was shocked when they found out. I'm still healing in the name of Jesus.*
>
> *It's been years, and I am even remarried; but the hurt and disappointment is still there at times. Just the enemy trying to get me down. I'm on to him though.*

If you're struggling to get the everyday things done, admit it! Don't hide. Don't tuck those bills away in a stack at the back of your closet. Don't line your hallway with unpacked boxes. Plan.

Organize. Get busy. You might be surprised to learn that you're better at taking care of business than you ever expected. If you make it a priority in your life, you will master those tasks, even the toughest ones.

Perhaps you've never had to do these things before. Maybe you don't know where to start. Begin at the beginning by asking yourself what needs doing. Write each one down as it occurs to you. Once you have a list, you will need to prioritize. What's most pressing? If that approach doesn't work, then find someone who can counsel you on where to start. Perhaps you have a friend who is an organizational whiz. You know, one of those wonderful women whose pantries are arranged alphabetically and whose closets are color-coded. Go to her. Ask for her help. Perhaps you will find you can return the favor. If not now, then sometime in the future.

According to Professional Life Coach Nancy Williams:

> *When we move through a major life transition, it often feels as though the ground beneath our feet—the foundation that provided security—has shifted. When a significant area of our lives changes, it seems as if our whole world has changed. We find ourselves on a new path we may or may not have chosen as we struggle to get our bearings and determine our next steps.*
>
> *Familiarity, self-care, and routine can help create a sense of stability and comfort that will enable us to adapt to change and move forward with our lives. Connecting with people, activities, and personal things that are familiar*

*reminds us that while part of our lives seems to have changed dramatically, other elements are still in place. Even the simplest of things like enjoying favorite foods, pets, hobbies, and time with friends remind us that we have not lost ourselves completely. Activities that nurture our bodies and our souls generate a level of comfort while meeting basic needs.*

*Routine helps establish a structure that fosters a sense of safety and stability. It also prevents us from drawing inward and pulling away from the very activities and relationships that will support us as we move forward. While we don't know what the future holds, we do know what we are to do one day at a time. Having a daily schedule is a significant early step in reorganizing our lives.*

Even the pros agree. . .things just won't get done unless you have a plan. So, what's on your to-do list? Do you need to deal with financial issues? Still working on dividing up your assets? Thinking about going back to school? Need to learn new skills? Looking for a godly counselor—for you and/or your kids? Struggling to keep up with laundry? Begin to plan ahead. Chart your course. Then watch as God undergirds your plan with the breath of His Spirit. He's not sitting back, you know. The Lord is taking an active role in your life. And He's not interested in seeing you grow stagnant. On the contrary, He wants you to run the race. So, reach for that baton, sister! Let's get going!

*I can do all things through Christ who strengthens me.*
PHILIPPIANS 4:13 NKJV

# GRACE IT

Just about the time you think you don't have it in you to get back to work, you stumble across a scripture like this from 2 Corinthians 9:8 (KJV): "And God is able to make all grace abound toward you; that ye, always having all sufficiency in all things, may abound to every good work."

"What's that?" you cry. "*All* sufficiency?" Does that really mean He will give you everything you need to get things done? Yep. Even when you're having a hard time believing it. *Especially* when you're having a hard time believing it. Sometimes God gives us the grace to do things on our own, and other times He sends people into our lives to assist His work. Be open to either as you allow the Lord to lead you through the maze toward the day when your recovery is complete.

Maybe you're the type who is always helping others. For you, this sufficiency thing is difficult. Allow God to show you how to release this area back to Him. Give Him the control He needs to make this part of your adjustment easier.

Don't give up! Get back in the game. Sure, you might struggle at times; but even in the struggles, God will give you what you need. Why not share your heart with Him today?

*Father, I'm so grateful for the healing You've already done in my life. I'm so glad that the fears are dissipating and that I can come to You in the Holy of Holies. I know it's time to get back to the business of living, but I sometimes find myself struggling. In spite of the accomplishments I've*

*made, I'm still tempted to crawl under the covers at times
and forget about the hard things. Can't I just take a bubble
bath for, say, a year? Or maybe a long winter's nap? Oh,
how wonderful that sounds. Still, I know in my heart that
You want me to take steps forward. I'm going to need Your
help. Thank You that Your grace gives me everything I need
. . .and more! Amen.*

## ⟳ ERASE IT

*Courage, sacrifice, determination, commitment, toughness,
heart, talent, guts. That's what little girls are made of;
the heck with sugar and spice.*
BETHANY HAMILTON

Okay, so you've admitted that getting back to work has been a
bit of a challenge. And some tasks are clearly harder than others.
You'll do better in some areas (say, going to your job every day)
before others (doing laundry, paying bills on the appropriate
days, etc.). It's okay. Acknowledging the weak areas can only
help you grow stronger. In order to erase your problems, you've
gotta face them!

Take a look at the following list and think about which ones
seem most overwhelming to you.

• Going to work every day

- Finding a job
- Moving/unpacking
- Taking care of the house
- Going back to school
- Switching things over to your name (bank accounts, utilities, etc.)
- Going to church (or any other place where you and your husband used to go as a couple)
- Carrying on a conversation
- Grocery shopping
- Doing laundry
- Cooking
- Organizing and paying bills
- Making good choices
- Eating
- Sleeping

Which of these tasks presents the biggest challenge? It might be a good idea to put them in order, with the toughest at the top and the easiest at the bottom. Feel free to add to the list. Likely, you have some hard-to-take-care-of tasks that have been overlooked here.

Once you have your list in hand, start at the bottom and work your way up. Begin by thanking the Lord for giving you those tasks to do. They are your friends, not your enemies. Then, as you approach the things on the top of the list, ask Him to give you wisdom for how to accomplish those things—in His time, and with His strength.

He will do this, and not in any small measure due to your abilities. Don't think because you don't feel capable that in any way this hinders God's purposes. Ask and you will receive. He promises it!

## ◯ REPLACE IT

*You can't turn back the clock—but you can wind it up again.*
ANONYMOUS

You've taken a good look at the tasks that are hardest to tackle. Now let's look at some practical ways to approach them, so that you can get back to the business of living.

- **Having trouble getting out of bed in the morning?** Struggling when you think about spending the day at work? Though you might not feel like it at the moment, your job is a gift. Instead of bemoaning the fact that you have to go to work, begin to praise the Lord for your job. Without it where would you be? Spend time every day thanking the Lord for your boss and your co-workers. Pray for each of them by name and ask God to bless not only the employees but also the company. Pray about the people you touch, the work you do, and even those who may cause some measure of grief during your day. Even those you pass on your daily commute are fodder for prayer. If they're stuck in the same traffic as you, they probably need it! You will find that as you train yourself to go to God first, your attitude will change. When you swing your legs over the edge of the bed, begin to speak positive things over your day, especially as it relates to your work.

- **Looking for a job?** If you're having trouble finding the perfect job, think about using the services of an employment agency. There are a few strings involved, but they have leads that you do not. If you're well connected online (part of a social network), let people there know, too. Many churches now have employment ministries that can put members in touch with job opportunities as well. Put together a great résumé, and then begin to pound on doors. Don't know how to dust off the résumé and give it a good polish? Get online and read up on tips from the experts or attend a job fair. The more doors you knock on, the more courageous you will be. And don't fret! God wants this process to be fun. You're about to meet new friends and learn new skills. Best of all, the Lord knows exactly where you're going to be working. . .and why. So, trust Him!

- **Having trouble keeping up with things at home?** There's really only one way to do this. You have to put yourself on a schedule and stick with it. If you're exhausted when you get home from work, then take the time you need to read a book, take a bubble bath, or watch TV. But set your timer to remind yourself to wash clothes, dishes, etc. Don't try to do it all in one day. That's too exhausting, and you may only meet with failure. Rather, give yourself a task or two per day to complete so that, at the end of the week, you're done and able to enjoy a stress-free weekend. Here's another fun way to get some work done while you're in rest mode: If you're in the middle of a great television show (even if it's your only time to zone out), make commercial time your work time. You'll be stunned at how much you can get done in the three-minute time frame, if you just jump to your feet and get busy! During the show you can fold clothes or sort mail, being sure to keep the shredder nearby. Between the times you're resting and the times you're racing the clock to finish before the commercials end, you should knock out your list in a show or two. Or put on a movie and spend the next hour and a half watching while doing whatever needs done in that particular room. Dust, mop, sweep, anything that will allow you to see the movie and still keep moving. It's amazing what you can do when you have a plan and a goal!

- **Thinking about going back to school?** What fun! Picking out your classes, wondering about the new things you'll learn, thinking about the friends you're sure to make. . .this one's not as tough as you might think. When you think about going back to school, use the words, "I get to" instead of "I have to." Those words will completely change your thinking! Whereas before you were consumed with all the things related to your husband and keeping the marriage going, now you're free to focus on what is best for the life you're going to lead. Then, begin to imagine the possibilities. Where will this education take you? Ideally to a better paying job and an exciting future. And while you're at it, think back to the dreams you had as a teenager. What did you want to be when you grew up? Did you consider law school or perhaps a career in nursing? Were there goals you set aside when you met and married your husband? You may have begun a career in a field you loved only to discover you had to make changes to adapt to your married state. Maybe you're like Judy:

> *During and after my divorce, I discovered I had a renewed passion for writing. I found I soon wanted to use my gift to help others by encouraging single parents and by telling my story so perhaps other people wouldn't have to go through the terrible pain and upheaval I went through. I threw myself into writing; and that, along with being a mom and a dog-owner, helped me get out of bed in the morning.*

Can you see how things you once enjoyed can be revived and used to help not only yourself but also others? So, dear sister in Christ, think. Pray. Remember. Go back to the days when you asked "what if?" What if you could be anything you wanted? Well, what's stopping you except the attempt? Maybe it's time to relight that fire!

- **If you're in the process of switching things over to**

**your name (bank accounts, utilities, etc.), then you have your hands full.** But even this can be exciting. Yes, it means the responsibility for paying these things now falls only to you, but it also means that you're beginning again. Let those applications and phone calls mark just that—a new and fresh beginning. Don't look at them as another chore to complete. Just remember to take everything in bite-sized pieces. Don't look at the whole of it, just do one task at a time. And don't expect to have everything in order right away. Give yourself one task per day. Or one per week, perhaps, depending on the pace at which you need to move.

- **Some women struggle to eat right in the months after a separation.** Try using a website like www.fitday. com. There, you will find a journal where you can plug in the foods you've eaten that day and the calories and carbohydrates involved. If you're not Internet savvy, then just make a simple list at the end of each day, writing down the foods you've eaten. That way, you can tell at a glance if you're not getting the proper nutrition. (And remember, if you overlook this area, you'll be a mess emotionally and psychologically. Good nutrition is key to overcoming the stresses of life.) Take a look at Monica's story:

> *After my divorce, I plunged into the depths of despair. I lost a significant amount of weight. One of the reasons I stayed home so much was because I*

*didn't want people to see my deteriorating condition. A friend finally convinced me to see a nutritionist. Thank God! She walked with me, hand in hand, giving me a plan of action I could live with. Getting healthy again (and getting the nutritional balance I needed), helped me in every area of my life. Before long, I had the energy to dive back into life. I'm not saying it was easy. There were days when I still wanted to slip back into old habits. Still, I held onto the promise of God that I would live and not die. After a while, however, I wasn't just content to live. I wanted to live an abundant life. And I am! Praise the Lord!*

- **If you're not keen on grocery shopping, consider a different approach.** Do a once-a-month major shopping day. That way you'll only have to shop for the little things (milk, bread, etc.) in between. You might consider joining a co-op, where things like fresh fruits and vegetables are delivered to your home. Another option would be online grocery shopping. Several grocery stores now offer this option, though during this time it's easy to rely on deliveries that allow you to remain far too secluded. It's better for you to use this time as an outing to get you back into the world of people. Regardless, you need a change of heart. Plan a menu and stick with it to the best of your ability. That way, you will not only get the nutrition you need, you'll have the ingredients to cook the things on your list. "Random" grocery shopping won't work, especially at this stage in your life. Just grabbing a few items and tossing them into your basket will not translate into a meal. In fact, you will find yourself eating out more than ever if you try this shot-in-the-dark approach. And as for considering this a chore, think of your trip to the grocery store as just one more thing that gets you out among people. Consider the fact that while you're checking off the items on your list, you're also taking one more step toward rejoining the world.

- **Organizing and paying bills.** If you're having trouble figuring out how to deal with your bills, don't be afraid to ask for help. It's possible your church has someone on staff who can help you with this. If not, ask around. See if your friends or family members can recommend someone they trust to assist you. Having an accountability partner is key. So is keeping your bills in one place. It's harder to pay them if you don't know where they are. There are many great bill organizers out there. Find one that works and promise yourself you will use it faithfully. The system of leaving things in stacks on your kitchen countertop or office desk won't work for you in this time of your life. You'll have to keep a close eye on your finances, but even this challenge can be a fun one if you approach it with a positive frame of mind. Take a look at Abby's story:

> *Months (and even years) after my divorce, I still*

*struggled in the area of bill-paying. I hated checking the mail and often just tossed the bills in the front seat of my car or in a pile on the kitchen cabinet. This led to a few mess-ups. More than once, I forgot to pay a bill. On a couple of other occasions, I got behind on credit cards. What a mess! It took a real financial shaking to convince me I needed a method to get through this. I bought a filing cabinet and decided to keep things in order. I set a certain day of the month as bill-paying day. I'm not saying things have always run smoothly, but I'm getting better. That's all I can ask of myself, really. Baby steps.*

- **Struggling with impulsive decisions?** Many women make decisions in the early stages when they're in shock and regret them later, wishing they could undo them. This is the time for an accountability partner. Prayerfully choose someone who can walk alongside you as you make major decisions—a good friend, a grown child, a parent, a spiritual leader. Then, before you make a big decision, run it by your accountability partner. Get his/her take on things before you make a move. You might not always agree, but at least you will have that second person's input. Also, make a point of praying over your decisions. Give yourself time to process all the information before jumping into anything important. Your time is worth taking when things are out of balance as they are now. You'll not regret moving slowly when it's all said and done.

> *Do not let what you cannot do*
> *interfere with what you can do.*
> JOHN WOODEN

## EMBRACE IT

Getting back to the business of living might be tough, but it's medicine to your weary soul. Keeping up with the daily stuff is a great way to keep your focus where it belongs. After all, who has time to fret over their woes when they're busy? And if you're like many women, the mere act of standing to your feet and doing something gives not only the benefit of having done something constructive but also, if the labor is physical, of getting out some measure of frustration.

Here's a nugget of truth: You are far stronger than you think you are. Don't believe it? Consider this: With the voice of the Holy Spirit to guide you and the power of the Lord resident within you, there is no mountain you can't climb. God is telling you that no matter how alone you feel, none of these tasks will be done as a solo effort. So, don't look at these things as impossible, or even hard. They are completely doable, with the help of your heavenly Father. Nothing—absolutely nothing—is impossible with Him.

As we close out this section, take a look at Natalie's story. Perhaps you will be able to relate.

*After nine years of being a stay-at-home mom, the thought of going back to work terrified me. I'd already been through one change with the breakup of the marriage. Now this? My youngest was two, and I felt like I was depriving her of what her two older sisters had taken for granted. But you do what you've got to do, right? It was up to me to provide for them now. That meant something had to give. I had to work.*

*Having been a secretary before, I wasn't worried. People always needed secretaries. I could type 50 words per minute and knew shorthand and ten-key. I perused the want ads, wondering what planet the newspaper was from. They said things like Word Perfect and Lotus 1-2-3. What was that? Ah yes, while I was enjoying mommydom, computers had come front and center in the workplace. I didn't know anything. I was a failure. My children would starve. Or so I thought.*

*Thanks to a wonderful job-placement company, I quickly learned that computers weren't quite as intimidating as I'd feared. As my skills increased, my attitude changed. Before long, I was at home in the office. However, I did learn that if you rest your fingers on the keys too hard, you end up with a page full of Ls.*

Don't you love Natalie's sense of humor? Sure, it's easy to see the conflict going on inside of her as she faced this strange new world, but she made the leap and even had the courage to laugh at herself. You're going to make it, too! Getting back to business is a necessity, and it's something you're going to do with God's hand in yours.

Take a look at the following scriptures as you ponder the

tasks ahead of you. Memorize them, as you are able, so that you will have them handy as needed.

- *For who is God, except the LORD? And who is a rock, except our God? It is God who arms me with strength, and makes my way perfect. He makes my feet like the feet of deer, and sets me on my high places.*
  PSALM 18:31–33 NKJV

- *Commit to the LORD whatever you do, and your plans will succeed.*
  PROVERBS 16:3 NIV

- *And let the beauty of the LORD our God be upon us, and establish the work of our hands for us; yes, establish the work of our hands.*
  PSALM 90:17 NKJV

God is so proud of you! You might not feel like you're accomplishing much; but the strides you're making, even the small ones, are huge in His sight. So, keep those feet moving. Put one in front of the other. And the road will stretch out before you, a beautiful path toward an exciting future in the Lord.

*The fact is, that to do anything in the world worth doing,*
*we must not stand back shivering and thinking of the cold and danger,*
*but jump in and scramble through as well as we can.*
ROBERT CUSHING

# Chapter 8

## *CONTENT IN HIM*

*We have no right to ask when sorrow comes,*
*"Why did this happen to me?" unless we ask the same question*
*for every moment of happiness that comes our way.*
UNKNOWN

# FACE IT

When you hear the word "contentment," what do you think of? A blissful state of mind? Leaning back in your easy chair, not a care in the world? Sitting in front of a fireplace on a winter's day with a book in your hand and a cup of hot tea at your side? Maybe it's a beach somewhere with an umbrella and a good book. Perhaps contentment is something you're not sure how to define. Oh, you believe in contentment because Jesus says it exists, but you're still waiting for that day to come.

Is it possible you've never actually considered what it is to be content? If you think contentment is having all you want, then you'll never find it. Rather, to be content is to want what you have. Sounds simple, but let's look at this concept in greater detail.

"How can I possibly be happy given all I've lost?" you ask. Perhaps you can't—yet—be happy, but happiness should never be confused with contentment.

Maybe you're of the mindset that contentment can't be achieved until your problems are behind you. Nothing could be further from the truth. Take a good look at these words from Philippians 4:11–13 (NKJV): "Not that I speak in regard to need, for I have learned in whatever state I am, to be content: I know how to be abased, and I know how to abound. Everywhere and in all things I have learned both to be full and to be hungry, both to abound and to suffer need. I can do all things through Christ who strengthens me."

If you want the real recipe for contentment, it's this: Don't wait until your problems are solved to shake off your discontentment. They never will be, as this was never meant to be a perfect life. Start today, regardless of what you're facing.

Maybe you read that and think, "Are you kidding? You don't know what I've been through!" Maybe your husband took off with another woman. Maybe you were abandoned, left to fend for yourself. Perhaps you're fighting to keep your head above water financially. Maybe you made monumental mistakes, costing you your marriage and your children. Contentment seems impossible. You find yourself saying things like, "Someday things will be different. Someday I'll be happy again. *Then* I'll be content. But not now. Impossible!"

Well, good news, sister! We serve the God of the impossible!

Fortunately for you—and millions of other women in your shoes—you can learn to be content in whatever state you are in. Despite your circumstances. Even if life hasn't turned out like you thought it would, you can still be content in Him. Yes, you've surely suffered some losses. Your world, as you knew it, has gone through a major shift. People, places, and things are not the same. Maybe you're in a smaller home, driving a car that's barely holding on. Perhaps you're struggling to pay bills or put food on the table. Likely, you can't afford pedicures or other such luxuries. Still, you can learn to be content. . .regardless of your situation.

One enemy of contentment is unforgiveness. If you're finding that you are discontent much of the time, maybe you still need to forgive your ex-husband or others who might have wronged you. You say you can't possibly forgive? Can't possibly get past the awful things your spouse has done? Forgiveness isn't an option; it's a command. Why not pause for a moment and seek the Lord about this matter? Then, when you're sure you've forgiven (to the best of your ability), return to finish the chapter.

Jay Meyers, Christian counselor, has this take on finding contentment despite circumstances:

> *"The past doesn't want to stay in your past," observed a therapist to the main character in the movie* The Kid. *And isn't it true of us? Our past doesn't want to stay in our past. It rears its ugly head in our anger at our children or in our blaming others for our mistakes or in beating ourselves up in the losing game of shame. We can travel down this dead-end road or take the exit of facing, admitting, and confessing our deep issues and struggles.*
>
> *It has been said that admitting the problem is half of the solution. I have seen this time and time again as a breakthrough point for struggling people on their way to healing. Recently a young man left my office where I just listened to him finally pour out buckets of his shameful sins, guilt, and fears. He thanked me for helping. All I did was listen. He faced the deep issues. He took the exit to freedom.*
>
> *This is not new. The scriptures have said it all along: "When I refused to confess my sin, my body wasted away, and I groaned all day long. Day and night your hand of discipline was heavy on me. My strength evaporated like water in the summer heat. Finally, I confessed all my sins to you and stopped trying to hide my guilt. I said to myself, 'I will confess my rebellion to the LORD.' And you forgave me! All my guilt is gone" (Psalm 32:3–5 NLT).*

All gone! Isn't that reason to profess not only thanks but also contentment that, while our situation isn't what we'd hoped or dreamed, it is in God's hands? It's under control.

Another enemy of contentment is anger. It's possible you're still angry with yourself or your spouse over what happened in your marriage. Sure, there were things he could have done differently. Maybe the fact that he didn't has you keyed up. And yes, there were plenty of things you could've done differently. Maybe your reactions weren't always what they should have been, for instance. What's done is done. It's in the past. Time to let that go.

Where would be the fairness in that, you might ask? How can you possibly pretend things did not happen? God isn't asking you to pretend. He is asking you to hand all the suffering, the pain and rejection, the hurtful words, the lies—all of it— over to the foot of the cross where Jesus Christ bore all of those things and more. He took your suffering to the cross where it remains unless you snatch it back.

Not a pretty picture is it, us grabbing right out of the hands of Jesus so we might hold onto something that's not ours to hold? It is a process, this act of forgiving; and even if you were mostly innocent in your divorce (there is no perfect spouse, so even if the blame is tiny, it's best to accept it now rather than deal with God on it later), you will need to start by forgiving yourself and then begin to work on forgiving your spouse. A word of warning: You cannot under any circumstances forgive someone apart from the strength of the Lord. It is impossible. So take those issues to the cross and nail them there. Then, hard as it seems, turn your back and leave them for Jesus to deal with. And He will. Then you will be truly free and able to find contentment in the present and to see the future that lies ahead.

Above all, contentment will only come when you accept the fact that the past is truly in the past. You are where you are. It's time to start living in the present. And who knows? The future might just surprise you!

After going through so many losses, Cindy began to struggle with discontentment. In fact, she carried around that unsettled feeling for quite some time before finally acknowledging the fact that she felt discontent. After facing this head-on, the shackles fell. She saw things for what they were. Somehow, the recovery process after the divorce had actually increased her faith. Oh, not at first. But eventually. When it came to contentment, she leaned on the verse: "Do not love the world nor the things in the world" (1 John 2:15 NASB). She developed an eternal viewpoint instead of a temporary one, and you can, too. As Cindy learned, it may seem difficult at first—even impossible; but with God everything is possible, *especially* contentment!

Take a look at this passage from 1 Timothy 6:6–9 (NKJV): "Now godliness with contentment is great gain. For we brought nothing into this world, and it is certain we can carry nothing out. And having food and clothing, with these we shall be content. But those who desire to be rich fall into temptation and a snare, and into many foolish and harmful lusts which drown men in destruction and perdition."

We own nothing. Think about that for a moment. Nothing in your possession is actually yours. Nothing. Not the car in your driveway, the pillow under your head at night, or the shoes in your closet. So, what does it matter how much stuff you collect or how big your house is? You won't be taking any of it with you to heaven. Who cares if you're eating steak or hamburger? Why does it matter if you drive a Lexus or a Chevy? Is it really such a big deal that you don't have a fancy house or expensive furnishings?

You can be content in a newer (and possibly smaller) home. You can be content with holidays being different from before. You can be content with "sleeping single in a double bed." You can be content as an unmarried person. How? By drawing near to the Lord. After all, the Bible says you're not alone! God wants to awaken you to His love (the ultimate love). Once you fully understand that love, contentment will wrap over you like a warm, fuzzy blanket.

God longs to give you an attitude of gratitude, whether your circumstances are good, bad, or otherwise. Truly, the only way to achieve contentment in this life is to submit to His will. To trust that He's giving you His best. He wants to convince you that your future is better than your past. In fact, He wants to convince you that your *present* is pretty good, too!

If you've been struggling in this area, don't beat yourself up. You're in good company. Many noted women in the Bible battled the same thing. Think about Gomer, Hosea's wife. She was rescued from a life of prostitution, brought into his home—a place of safety and comfort (and a far cry from her old life)—and given the place of a favored wife. But Gomer didn't make the adjustment well. Her discontentment with the new life caused her to sneak back over the wall and return to her former ways. (Can you relate?) And what about Martha, one of the New Testament's most talked-about females? When Jesus came to her home for a visit, she expressed serious discontentment with her sister, accusing her of not working hard enough. Can you imagine it? Mary was sitting at the feet of Jesus absorbing the teachings of the Master while Martha was stirring the soup and fretting about who would set the table. In reality, Mary had the better idea!

Both of these women had to come to an understanding of contentment, and so do you. Contentment is a choice. . .and it's one you can make today.

## GRACE IT

In order to be content, you need to be "settled." In other words, you have to make up your mind that no matter what comes your way, you won't let it shake you. Think about the words of 1 Peter 5:10 (KJV): "But the God of all grace, who hath called us unto his eternal glory by Christ Jesus, after that ye have suffered a while, make you perfect, stablish, strengthen, settle you."

Don't you love those three *S*s? We are stablished (found, accepted, recognized, secure), strengthened, and settled. Ponder that last one for a moment. The same "amazing grace" you've sung about all your life actually calms your spirit, giving you that "settled" feeling. Do you think about that—about contentment—when you hear those words? Next time, perhaps you should, because clearly, grace and contentment go hand in hand. Why not spend a little time talking with God about that?

> *Lord, I've always known Your grace was (and is) amazing. Today I'm more thankful than ever. You're "settling" me, Father. Making me content. I lay aside any self-pity, any anger over things not going my way. I give this area of my life over to You. Help me deal with every issue that has stirred up discontentment. Settle me, Lord, with Your awesome, life-changing grace! Amen.*

## ERASE IT

> *I'm not telling you it is going to be easy—*
> *I'm telling you it's going to be worth it.*
> ART WILLIAMS

In order to rid yourself of discontentment, you have to take a look at what's causing it. Maybe you're not even sure why you have that "unsettled" feeling so much of the time. Take a look at the following things to see if they resonate with you.

What am I discontent with?

- My lowered status/loss of former world
- The unfairness of my situation
- Where I live

- That my ex-husband is happy (Ouch! There's that forgiveness issue!)
- The amount of responsibility I have to take on
- The inability to fix things in the house on my own
- The fact that my children enjoy their time with my ex-husband and/or his new wife
- The changes I've been through (and am still going through)
- Lack of knowledge about the future
- My lack of male companionship
- My bank balance
- What I see in the mirror
- My reactions
- My job or lack of it
- My poor attitude

Ultimately, discontentment arises from a feeling that you've somehow been cheated out of something. . .that you deserve better. Deserve more. However, even if your circumstances don't change, your heart can. God longs for you to let go of the "what ifs" and focus on the things He's done—and continues to do—in your life.

# CREPLACE IT

*As the deer pants for streams of water, so my soul pants for you,*
*O God. My soul thirsts for God, for the living God.*
*When can I go and meet with God?*
PSALM 42:1–2 NIV

It's time to replace some of that discontentment with contentment from on-high. But how do you go about that? It all comes down to relationship. No, not relationship with a man. Relationship with *the* Man.

The answer to all contentment issues is found in 1 Timothy 6:6 (KJV): "But godliness with contentment is great gain." The only way you will ever understand contentment is if you come to understand godliness. And the only way to understand godliness is to actually spend time with God, to glean from Him, to learn His ways.

Maybe you were accustomed to getting your own way before the divorce. It's time to admit that getting your own way, while fun at times, isn't necessarily God's plan for success. His ways are so much higher than our own; and His thoughts, so much grander! We can trust Him with the roadmap of our lives.

God longs for you to be content in Him. Nothing else. Just Him. Ponder those words. It's you and Jesus now. It's time to stop saying, "Why can't You do things my way, Lord?" and start saying, "Lord, lead me in Your ways. I will walk in them with a contented heart."

Here are ten great reasons you can walk in contentment:

1. God loves you. In fact, He adores you.
2. God started a good work in you. . .and He plans to finish it.
3. Jesus paid it all. (He's walked ahead of you and is waiting for you there.)
4. God can change whatever needs to be changed (the situation, your heart, etc.).
5. God is your provider and knows what you need.
6. God can and will use your testimony to touch others.
7. What the enemy meant for evil, God will use for good.
8. Being single gives you time to genuinely focus on the Lord, the true source of contentment.
9. God's ways are higher than yours.
10. You are the bride of Jesus. You have the best husband in the world. He's incapable of hurting you, cheating on you, or breaking your heart.

If you're honest with yourself, you'd have to admit that most discontentment comes from spending too much time thinking about your own situation. Inward focus generally leads to a fetal position, the inability to see past your own pain. The more you fill your mind with thoughts of your own situation, the less room there is for God. Outward focus always leads to seeing things in perspective, looking at your situation in the grand scheme of things. So, as painful as this realization might be, if most of your conversations with friends start with the words *I*, *me*, or *my*, you might need a focus shift.

The following list will help you turn your focus to others.

Talk about the perfect remedy for discontentment!

Ten Ways to Shift Your Focus:

1. **Perform at least one random act of kindness every day.** Perhaps you're good at organizing or have extra time on your hands. Offer your services to the care ministry at church or sign up to read to a child through an after-school program. Resolve to make one person smile every day. Make it your personal challenge. Or perhaps you like to write. Write a thank-you note to one person every day. If costs are a factor, use postcards to cut down on the mailing rate. Let someone know you appreciate them, even if it's just the checker at the grocery store or the man who delivers the mail. "Like apples of gold in settings of silver is a word spoken in right circumstances" (Proverbs 25:11 NASB).

2. **Bless the poor.** Give, even if it's out of your lack. You may not have the funds to go beyond your monthly tithe, but perhaps you can make sandwiches to hand out to the homeless or spend a day volunteering at a shelter or soup kitchen. Any time spent in doing good is not wasted, and you will profit much more than those who receive. "He who is kind to the poor lends to the LORD, and he will reward him for what he has done" (Proverbs 19:17 NIV).

3. **Develop an attitude of gratitude.** Don't forget to give God thanks, even in the bad times. Did you wake

up this morning? Praise the Lord. Do you have a roof over your head, even a leaking one? Thank You, Jesus. Perhaps you were delayed on your way to work this morning due to a flat tire or a dead battery. Could it be you missed out on a major accident with that delay? Choose to believe God kept you from potential harm, and you'll see how it is possible to thank Him even for automobile issues. "Let the word of Christ dwell in you richly as you teach and admonish one another with all wisdom, and as you sing psalms, hymns and spiritual songs with gratitude in your hearts to God" (Colossians 3:16 NIV).

4. **Go on a missions trip or participate in local missions.** There's nothing like getting a fresh perspective. When combined with the fact you're also offering help, a missions trip is a place of bountiful blessings—for all parties. "And he said unto them, Go ye into all the world, and preach the gospel to every creature" (Mark 16:15 KJV).

5. **Read the Sermon on the Mount.** Often. Savor every word. Cherish them. Vow daily to put the words of our Savior into practice. Jesus knew what you would need, and He's provided ample help for any hurts in these passages. "Now when he saw the crowds, he went up on a mountainside and sat down. His disciples came to him, and he began to teach them" (Matthew 5:1–2 NIV).

6. **Feed the hungry.** Cook meals for shut-ins or deliver Meals On Wheels. Give to your local food pantry, even

if you don't have much to give. Your "not so much" can be another's bounty. "For I was hungry and you gave me something to eat, I was thirsty and you gave me something to drink, I was a stranger and you invited me in" (Matthew 25:35 NIV).

7. **Volunteer in the children's ministry.** If that doesn't work, pray about a particular ministry where you can share your gifts with others. Often the need is great and the volunteers are few. "Jesus said, 'Let the little children come to me, and do not hinder them, for the kingdom of heaven belongs to such as these'" (Matthew 19:14 NIV).

8. **Befriend an elderly person, even offering to clean her home, if appropriate.** Warning: You might think you're the one doing the favor, but in the end you will see that the wisdom she shares with you provides the greater blessing. "Pure and genuine religion in the sight of God the Father means caring for orphans and widows in their distress and refusing to let the world corrupt you" (James 1:27 NLT).

9. **Become a student of the Word.** Learn passages and commit them to memory. Study the words, then go deeper to seek out their meaning. If you can afford it, find a good Bible concordance or invest in a study Bible. The more you dig, the more of the Lord's bounty and grace there is to find. "For the word of God is quick, and powerful, and sharper than any twoedged sword, piercing even to the dividing asunder of soul and spirit, and of the joints and marrow, and is a discerner of the

thoughts and intents of the heart" (Hebrews 4:12 KJV).

10. **Praise God through every circumstance, even when it's hard.** Have you developed a thankful heart? Ask God to bless you with one. He will! Start with finding one thing each day to be thankful for, even if it is something small. Perhaps you would find it helpful to start a thankfulness journal where you can begin to record the things you're thankful for. As you grow more accustomed to this way of thinking, you will soon find there will be many, many more things to thank the Lord for each day. And as the number grows, so will your contentment. "I will praise thee, O Lord my God, with all my heart: and I will glorify thy name for evermore" (Psalm 86:12 KJV).

Now that you've read this list, make one of your own. What other things could you do to shift your focus outward? Write a note to your pastor to tell him what a great job he's doing? Get in touch with a relative you haven't connected with in years? Purchase a small gift for a loved one—just because—and wrap it in special paper and ribbons? The possibilities are endless. Once you begin to turn your focus to others, you will find that discontentment flees! There's just something about caring for others—even during your roughest season—that fills your heart with contentment.

# EMBRACE IT

It really *is* possible to have a contented heart, even during seasons that would otherwise bring on discontentment. You *can* have that settled feeling if you are willing to put in the heartwork it takes to get it. Practice thankfulness. Deal with the things that need to be dealt with, then shift your focus to others. Don't let the *I-me-my*s consume you.

Take a look at Jenny's story. Perhaps you can relate to her journey out of discontentment.

> I wasn't content in my marriage, and I wasn't content in my divorce. Strange, I know. But discontentment drove me. I couldn't see past myself at times.
>
> When the marriage ended, I had to come to grips with the fact that the only way I could shake the discontentment was to start all over again, to give my heart to the Lord. When I did that, my whole focus changed. I was suddenly content, not in my outward circumstances, but in Him.
>
> I allowed the Lord to bring new experiences, new relationships. About this same time, I started attending a new church, filled with people who extended the hand of love in my direction. Before long, I joined a Bible study. Then the choir. Soon enough, I was delivering Meals On Wheels. Then I decided to help out in the nursery. Before long, I went on a missions trip to Ecuador.
>
> My second phase of life was actually far more adventurous than my first, because it took me out of my comfort

*zone and into a world filled with people who loved me.*
*Through it all, God convinced me that loving Him is truly*
*the only way to lasting contentment.*

Can you see the key to Jenny's healing? Contentment came when she turned her focus outward. Only then did she realize God's true calling on her life. And once she settled into that call, all of her former discontentment faded away.

Now take a look at Carol's story. She allowed the Lord to take her discontentment and use it as a catalyst to reach out to women in her community.

*Of course, I was discontent! I'd lost everything of value to*
*me except my kids, and they weren't exactly making me smile*
*during those transition months either. I'd been left with all*
*the work while my ex got all the fun.*

*One weekend while he had the kids, I began to shout at*
*God. I mean, really yell. (Thank goodness for the thick walls*
*at my condo else the cops would have probably been called!)*
*I asked Him what in the world I was good for now—what*
*possible purpose I could be used for, given my broken state.*

*When I ran out of words, I just sat down in the middle*
*of the tiny living room on the ratty carpet and prepared for*
*round two. Then I heard it: silence. It was so quiet it echoed*
*in that room. I spied my Bible and reached for it (not a far*
*stretch in the small space). Wouldn't you know the verse I*
*opened to was the one about caring for the widows? I had*
*to laugh because I live in a complex that's full of older ladies*

*whose husbands have passed on.*

*I remember closing the Bible and praying for the opportunity to help those women; and even as I said the words, I "knew" nothing would come of it. Suffice it to say I was wrong. It's been a year since then, and those ladies have become like family. My kids laugh about the number of choices they have to bring to school for grandparents day. Best of all, I don't hear the silence anymore. Now it's filled, and so am I.*

It's possible to turn your focus toward others in such a way that your own problems and anxieties fade into the background. Ask God to help you with this, to guide you under His power and in His direction, and He will! Best of all, when you spend your days caring for the needs of others, you are truly Christ's hand extended. There is no greater calling for the woman of God.

Take a good look at the following scriptures. They're sure to toss your lingering discontentment out the window!

- *I'm thanking you, God, from a full heart, I'm writing the book on your wonders. I'm whistling, laughing, and jumping for joy; I'm singing your song, High God.*
  PSALM 9:1–2 MSG

- *For none of us lives to himself alone and none of us dies to himself alone.*
  ROMANS 14:7 NIV

- *And having food and clothing, with these we shall be content.*
  1 TIMOTHY 6:8 NKJV

- *This vision is for a future time. It describes the end, and it will be fulfilled. If it seems slow in coming, wait patiently, for it will surely take place. It will not be delayed."*
  HABAKKUK 2:3 NLT

Child of God, it is possible to learn to be content in whatever state you are in. If your current state/situation is troubling, you will only exaggerate the problem by hanging on to any unforgiveness and discontentment. That's exactly what the enemy wants, which should be enough to convince you it's time to let it all go.

Here's a fun exercise to help you do just that. Pulling from the list above, write down all of the things that steal your contentment. Pray over each one. Then do one of two things with your list. Either burn or shred it (what fun!), or send it sailing off into space in a helium balloon. Either way, you're stating to yourself (and anyone who might be watching) that you're finally ready to let go.

*Contentment is a pearl of great price,*
*and whoever procures it at the expense of ten thousand desires,*
*makes a wise and a happy purchase.*
JOHN BALGUY

# Chapter 9

# LEANING ON GOD

*I love the use of the word "leaning." Faith is not just believing*
*in God and His faithfulness to do what He said, but in so completely*
*believing and trusting that you lean on Him and His Word*
*to the point that if He wasn't there, you'd fall.*
THOMAS BROOKS

# ⊂ FACE IT

When you hear the words *leaning on God*, what image comes to mind? Do you see yourself in an exhausted state, reaching out to the Lord just as you're about to cave in? Do you envision yourself much like a ladder, propped against the side of a building, hoping it holds? Maybe you can't even envision it at all. Perhaps the idea of leaning on anyone or anything, especially an invisible God, is foreign to you.

If you're like most people, you need to be propped up every now and again; but leaning on God is so much more than just running to Him when times are bad. Leaning on Him means resting in Him. Relying on Him. And that only comes out of relationship with Him.

Consider these verses from John 13:23–25 (MSG): "One of the disciples, the one Jesus loved dearly, was reclining against him, his head on his shoulder. Peter motioned to him to ask who Jesus might be talking about. So, being the closest, he said, 'Master, who?' "

These verses are referring to John, the disciple who would go on to be known as the disciple "Jesus loved dearly." What a great way to be remembered, as one who intimately loves—and is loved by—the Lord.

Remember that old hymn "Leaning on the Everlasting Arms"? There is safety in that place. There is fellowship in that place. There is joy divine in that place. There is trust—the kind that is birthed out of love—in that place. Think about that as you examine this verse in its fullness: "Trust in the LORD with all thine heart; and lean not unto thine own understanding" (Proverbs 3:5 KJV). When we lean on Him (as opposed to leaning on our own understanding), we are exhibiting trust. It's not shameful to admit we need to lean on the God of the universe. It's simple obedience.

Beloved, God adores you! You are "the one Jesus loves dearly." And He longs for you to rest your head on His shoulder, not just when you're going through troubles, but even when times are good.

Think about all of the many people throughout history who've had to lean on God. . .not just biblical heroes, but women of faith throughout the generations. Remember Fanny Crosby, the great hymn writer, who penned "Blessed Assurance"? She was blind from childhood but didn't let that stop her from writing more than two thousand songs of praise to her King. (Talk about learning to lean!) And what about Corrie ten Boom, who was imprisoned for hiding the Jews during Hitler's reign? Though she went through unbelievable horrors in a concentration camp, she leaned on her Savior and He carried her through. Her testimony touched—and continues to touch— millions. Contemplate the life of Mother Teresa. Did she not have to lean on Jesus as she carried out her work in the slums of Calcutta? Surely no one is better known for her intimate relationship with the King of kings.

Leaning on Jesus requires asking for wisdom and discernment, not just when you're going through your divorce, but every day thereafter. Let the words of James 1:2–5 (NASB) lead you: "Consider it all joy, my brethren, when you encounter various trials, knowing that the testing of your faith produces endurance. And let endurance have its perfect result, so that you may be perfect and complete, lacking in nothing. But if any of you lacks wisdom, let him ask of God, who gives to all generously and without reproach, and it will be given to him."

Pam Farrel, author of *Fantastic After 40*, offers this insight to help women peel back the layers on that verse:

> *When we ask for wisdom, wisdom to know God better, wisdom for the next step on the journey, wisdom to know what to do. . .God will give it. He gives it without reproach, meaning He won't mock us for asking or belittle our spirituality for asking. He will never say, "Come on. You should know this by now!" Nope. That is not in His nature. Compassion is.*
>
> *Verse 5 also says God gives wisdom "generously," like a rich cake piled high with luscious sweet frosting. When we quit asking Why? Why me? Why now? Why this? And instead ask for wisdom, God reframes the pain and we can move into the Promised Land of hope where He transforms our painful situations into something worthwhile.*[3]

Let's take one last look at Cindy. She dealt with many of the issues that you're familiar with. Her initial reaction to the divorce was to hide away, to pretend it hadn't happened. Fear gripped her and she felt stuck, like she couldn't put one foot in front of the other. She often wondered if she could go on.

---

[3] Pam Farrel, *Fantastic After 40*, Harvest House Publishers, 2007. Used with permission.

Fortunately, Cindy faced her fears head-on and eventually found the help she needed. Where? In the Holy of Holies. There, she allowed the Lord to do a deep work in her heart. She asked Him to root out the bitterness and pain, and gave Him permission to peel away the veneer.

The healing she acquired (which came as a result of seeking God daily for His will) eventually gave her the courage and the tenacity to enter the land of the living once again. Once there, she acquired new friendships, newfound faith, and an abundance of courage. She began to make choices—some good, some not so good—but learned from her mistakes. Before long, she was back in the groove, leading a healthy, happy life.

Ultimately, it was Cindy's relationship with Jesus that made the difference. Without Him—her true husband—she would likely have remained a victim, not a victor. Because of Him—because she learned to recline her head against His shoulder and to ask for wisdom in every circumstance—she rose above those circumstances and went on to do great things.

Lean on God, dear sister. He's the only one you can count on. He knows what you've been through, and He cares. God won't let you down. He's the husband you've always longed for, and He loves you like no other. He will provide for you. . . exceedingly, abundantly above all you could ask or think. He will pour out wisdom and discernment when you ask and will walk with you, hand in hand, through life's trials.

Best of all, He adores you. You are his precious bride, the love of His life. Oh, the joy of such a relationship! He is your safe place, a shoulder you can lean upon. And He longs for you to run to Him. . .today and always.

*Every thing that a man leans upon but God, will be a dart that will certainly pierce his heart through and through. He who leans only upon Christ lives the highest, choicest, safest, and sweetest life.*
THOMAS BROOKS

## GRACE IT

You've been through much more than you ever dreamed you were capable of. Ponder that for a moment. You probably never imagined yourself strong enough to survive the things you have. And yet, with God's hand in yours, you've come out a victor.

Contemplate the role grace has played in that journey. It is the very grace of God—His unmerited favor—that has wooed you into His presence. And there, in His presence, you have found (and will continue to find) the healing you need.

Take a close look at 2 Peter 3:18 (KJV): "But grow in grace, and in the knowledge of our Lord and Saviour Jesus Christ. To him be glory both now and for ever. Amen."

From the day you first trusted in Christ, you've been leaning on His grace. And talk about a growth spurt! You've been growing like a weed! Yes, you've come a long way, baby. . .but it's not time to stop now. No, the journey is merely beginning! So hang on for the ride!

*Lord, I feel like I've learned so much. Thank You for*

*Your unmerited favor. I'm so grateful for the growth that has taken place in my life. Lord, remind me daily to come into Your presence, that I might continue the journey, leaning fully on You. Amen.*

## ☾ EMBRACE IT

Do you sense the excitement ahead? God is doing amazing things. Leaning on Jesus will give you the strength you need. The power of the Holy Spirit lives inside you!

And guess what? Your happily-ever-after is more than just a fairy story in a book. It's a very real tale with a prince—*the* Prince—on a white horse, coming to sweep you away to a life of contentment, joy, and peace.

Don't you love that picture? Oh, daughter of God, such thrilling days lie ahead! As you lean on God, expect Him to restore your joy, the "pressed down, shaken together and running over" kind. Divorce or no divorce. . .joy is still yours for the taking. It is found in journeying with a loving God, reclining your head on His shoulder, and allowing Him to help you face whatever obstacles might come along. It's also found in delighting yourself in Him as He sweeps you away into the Holy of Holies, where He whispers words of love over you and gives you the desires of your heart.

Get ready to shout it from the rooftops! *On the tail end of every sorrow, there is a joyful tomorrow!* You, precious woman of

God, are living proof of that!

> *A bend in the road is not the end of the road. . .*
> *unless you fail to make the turn.*
> UNKNOWN

RESOURCES

WEB SITES/ORGANIZATIONS

**Divorce Care**
www.divorcecare.com
Help and healing for the hurt of separation and divorce

**Woman's Divorce**
www.womansdivorce.com
Divorce advice and help for women

**Christian Divorce Services**
www.christiandivorceservices.com
Resources for Christians facing divorce

**Fresh Start Seminars**
www.freshstartseminars.org
Divorce Recovery

**Christian Divorce Recovery**
www.walkingthechristianlife.com
Resources for people who've been through divorce

**Seasoned Sisters**
www.seasonedsisters.com
Making life fantastic after forty

# COUNSELORS

**Nancy Williams, M.Ed, LPC**
Counseling, Coaching, and Consulting Services
1521 Green Oak Place, Suite 120,
Kingwood, TX 77339
(281) 358-6654
www.nancywilliams.net

**White Stone Psychiatry**
Paul Looney, MD
26203 Oak Ridge Dr
The Woodlands, TX 77380
(281) 367-8255
www.looneydoc.com

# SUGGESTED READING

**My Utmost for His Highest**
By Oswald Chambers
Barbour Publishing

**Fantastic After 40**
By Pam Farrel
Harvest House Publishers

**Power Prayers for Women**
By Jackie M. Johnson
Barbour Publishing

**Everyday Joy**
By Janice Hanna
Barbour Publishing

**Bible Promise Book for Women**
Barbour Publishing

**199 Promises of God**
Barbour Publishing

**When "I Do" Becomes "I Don't"**
By Laura Petherbridge
David C. Cook, publisher

**When the Vow Breaks: A Survival and Recovery Guide for Christians Facing Divorce**
By Joseph Warren Kniskern and Steve Grissom
B&H Publishing

**Live, Laugh, Love Again: A Christian Woman's Survival Guide to Divorce**
By Carla Sue Nelson, Connie Wetzell, Michelle Borquez, Rosalind Spinks-Seay, Dr. Tim Clinton
Faithwords

**When He Leaves: Help and Hope for Hurting Wives**
By Kari West and Noelle Quinn
Harvest House

**Moving Forward After Divorce: Practical Steps to Healing Your Hurts**
By David Frisbie and Lisa Frisbie
Harvest House

**Men Who Hate Women and the Women Who Love Them**
*(When Loving Hurts and You Don't Know Why)*
by Susan Forward
Bantam

**Daily Spiritual Refreshment Bible for Women**
Barbour Publishing

# ABOUT THE AUTHORS

KATHLEEN Y'BARBO, bestselling author, publicist, and proud mother of a daughter and three grown sons, lives near Houston, Texas.

Author of over thirty Christian books, JANICE HANNA (aka Janice Thompson) is a "single-again" empty-nester who has already raised four godly daughters and now enjoys spending time with her three beautiful granddaughters.

Also available

# TURNING POINTS

## Whose Kids *are* These?

REDISCOVERING LOVE AND
LAUGHTER AS A STEP-MOM
by Karon Phillips Goodman

## The House is Quiet, *Now* What?

REDISCOVERING LIFE AND ADVENTURE AS
AN EMPTY NESTER
by Janice Hanna & Kathleen Y'Barbo

## Let the Crow's Feet and Laugh Lines Come!

REDISCOVERING BEAUTY
AND SELF-WORTH AT ANY AGE
by Dena Dyer

Available wherever books are sold.